# THE FOUNDATIONS OF WISDOM

VOLUME 4

# ETHICS

# THE FOUNDATIONS OF WISDOM

VOLUME 4

# ETHICS

FR. SEBASTIAN WALSHE, O. PRAEM.

TAN Books
Gastonia, North Carolina

Cover design by Andrew Schmalen

Library of Congress Control Number: 2023930696

ISBN: 978-1-5051-2645-7
Kindle ISBN: 978-1-5051-3180-2
ePUB ISBN: 978-1-5051-3181-9

Published in the United States by
TAN Books
PO Box 269
Gastonia, NC 28053
www.TANBooks.com

Printed in the United States of America

# CONTENTS

PREFACE

# Hunting for Happiness

The discovery and development of philosophy are part of man's larger search for happiness. As man was hunting for happiness, he found philosophy. Most of human ingenuity and energy was originally directed toward removing the obstacles to happiness: for example, the arts of hunting and agriculture were developed to alleviate hunger; the art of housebuilding was developed to alleviate the suffering associated with excessive heat and cold; various martial arts and weapons were developed to protect against violence from animals and other men; and medicine was developed to cure illness. But once these arts had been developed, and man had time for leisure, it became apparent that there exists in man a more fundamental desire than food, clothing, and bodily health. It is a desire not merely to avoid evil but a desire for some positive good, and it is a desire for a positive good that is not merely instrumental to something else (such as practical knowledge) but a good desired for its own sake. Aristotle expressed this desire simply in the statement, "All men by nature desire to know."[1]

It may seem strange that happiness should have much to do with knowledge. After all, very few men dedicate real effort and time to

1 Aristotle, *Metaphysics*, Bk. 1, Part I (hereinafter *Metaphysics*).

searching for knowledge. And what knowledge they do search for tends to be practical in nature—that is, it is for the sake of making or doing things. And yet, it is an indisputable fact of history that once the chief practical arts had been established and the needs of the body provided for, men naturally turned to philosophy in their leisure time. Aristotle recounts that "after all such arts had been developed, those sciences were pursued which are sought neither for the sake of pleasure nor necessity. This happened in places where men had leisure. Hence the mathematical arts originated in Egypt where the priestly class was permitted leisure."[2] And again, "When nearly all the things necessary for life, leisure and learning were acquired, this kind of prudence began to be sought."[3] But, if this is so, how do we account for the fact that so few people consider knowledge to be essential for happiness?

This question is like the question: Why do so few children prefer a high-paying job or an excellent education to ice cream? First, since the goods of the body are better known than the goods of the soul, it is natural that men should seek to provide for the goods of the body first. Second, happiness is not found in the possession and exercise of just any knowledge but in the best knowledge. And this is very difficult to achieve. Just as it would be impossible for a child to perform well at a high paying job or receive an excellent education all at once, it would be impossible for someone to acquire and use the knowledge needed for happiness without first passing through years of experience and study. Finally, notice that Aristotle did not say all men by nature desire to *come to* know but rather that all men by nature desire to know. Samuel Johnson, after seeing a famous landmark in Ireland, famously quipped that

---

[2] *Metaphysics*, 981b22–24; independent confirmation of the leisure afforded the priestly class in Egypt is found in Genesis 47:22.

[3] *Metaphysics*, 982b22–23.

it was "worth seeing . . . but not worth going to see."[4] There is a similar relationship between knowing and coming to know. Coming to know can be arduous and even painful. But if you asked the man on the street whether he would like to know some important truth if it took no effort, I suppose nearly everyone would say yes. But as it is, because many obstacles stand in the way of possessing knowledge, there are few who seek it.

So philosophy is near the end of man's search for happiness. But even within philosophy itself, there is an order of discovery that naturally arises from the search for happiness. We want to know the supreme good of man. But to know that, we need to know what man is, and since man is a natural being, we need to know what nature is. So philosophers began to examine nature. But once these things had been worked out in outline, it became clear that the nature of man is difficult to know, that it is even difficult to know about the existence and nature of the soul, and that the highest perfection of the human soul, wisdom, is even more difficult to know. Therefore, it was necessary to develop one final art, logic, which assists us in coming to know difficult truths well. Plato's Socrates seems to have been the first to acknowledge a need for an "art about arguments" in the *Phaedo*, precisely as he is searching to discover the existence and nature of the human soul.

The order of discovery in philosophy is almost inverse to the order in which philosophy should be learned. First, students should study logic, which is the art that treats of acquiring the good of speculative reason: truth. Therefore, since every science searches for truth, logic teaches how to proceed correctly in every science. Second, they should study mathematics, which among the sciences is the easiest in which to find certitude; there is

[4] James Boswell, *The Life of Samuel Johnson, LL.D.* (1791).

much agreement in this part of philosophy. Third, they should study natural things (natural philosophy). Fourth, among natural things, they should focus their study on living things, especially man (the study of the soul). Fifth, once they know accurately the nature of man and the various powers and perfections of the soul, they should study the good for man (ethics). And since man's supreme good consists in knowing things better than himself, the philosopher should study the first causes of all being (wisdom or metaphysics) last.[5] For the very exercise of knowing these things higher than man is the happiness that man desires. That is, natural happiness consists in contemplating the truths that are the conclusions of metaphysics.

Because this is only an introduction to philosophy, this text will not consider the last part of philosophy (metaphysics). Such a consideration belongs not to the beginning student but to an advanced student. Moreover, because the science of mathematics is widely taught and much easier than the other parts of philosophy, this text will not consider that part of philosophy either. Perhaps the best elementary treatment of mathematics, according to its proper method, can be found in Euclid's *Elements*.

Finally, this text will not proceed in a primarily historical method, as is typical in most introductions to philosophy. The order of history in philosophy is not necessarily a progression from ignorance to knowledge or error to truth. It is quite possible for an earlier philosopher to know more than a later one. Nor is the order of history necessarily the best order for the beginning student to follow if he is in search of truth. This text does not seek to inform the student about the positions taken by various philosophers

[5] This order of study is laid out by St. Thomas Aquinas at the beginning of his *Commentary on Aristotle's Nicomachean Ethics* and at the beginning of his *Commentary on the Book of Causes*.

but rather to lay out the method best suited to human nature of coming to understand the order among the ultimate causes of reality. We study the Pythagorean Theorem not to know that Pythagoras thought, but because it is true and worth knowing. And it would be worthwhile to study the same theorem even if it was discovered by Frankie Watkins. In philosophy, we are not so much concerned with who discovered some truth as with the truth itself and the reasons why it can be known. So while much of what is found in this text will be truths discovered by Aristotle and St. Thomas Aquinas, they stand on their own and do not rely upon the authority of those who first discovered and presented them.

INTRODUCTION

# The Art of Living Well

This fourth volume of *The Foundations of Wisdom* is dedicated to the study of ethics: the art of acting or living well. As we begin this last volume, it is good to look back upon what we have done so far and see how it has prepared us for the study of ethics. Recall that in the first volume (logic), we distinguished between practical and speculative knowledge. Practical knowledge is about an order that reason puts into things, while speculative knowledge is about an order that reason discovers in things. Recall, too, that the order reason puts into things depends upon the order reason discovers in things. For example, to put the form of a skyscraper into some material presupposes I have come to know the properties of some material capable of bearing such heavy weight (steel will do, but wood will not).

Two important truths follow from ethics being an art, i.e., a practical science. First, ethics is ordered to making or doing. The things we will study in ethics are not known simply for their own sake, any more than the recipes in a cookbook or the numbers in a phone book are to be known for their own sake. The knowledge you acquire from studying ethics must be used and applied to ordering your actions (specifically, your choices). Just knowing these truths will not make you good. Second, the order that reason puts into human acts depends upon an order that reason discovers, namely the order discovered in human nature and especially in the soul. This is why we studied the human soul before studying ethics. And since the human soul is a natural, substantial form, we had to study natural philosophy before studying the soul. And since the common road to follow in any science is determined by logic, it was necessary to study logic first. (Imagine, for example, trying to define the soul without having studied the art of defining.) So, looking back, we can see why we had to study these subjects in the order we did.

We saw in natural philosophy that every agent acts for an end, for some goal. (Remember that an agent cause is a moving cause, and there is no such thing as motion in no direction, so every agent must act toward some goal or direction). Human agents are no exception. All of our actions are for the sake of some goal. This becomes obvious from induction as well. Why did I pick up my philosophy book before class? So I could read it in class. Why did I pick up a plate and a fork and a knife in the lunch line? So I would have something on which to put my food and something with which to eat it. So all of our actions are for the sake of some end. And an action is judged to be better or worse based on how well that action actually brings someone to that intended end. If my end is to hit a baseball, and my action involves holding the bat on the wrong end or with my teeth or standing with my back to the pitcher, then that action is not a very good way of achieving my end.

Now, since ethics is the art of acting or living well, it is not concerned with just any limited end but with the ultimate goal or end of human life: the purpose of life. Therefore, ethics first will be concerned about identifying the ultimate end or ends of human life and then about determining the best or right means to that end. When all is said and done, the aim of ethics is to make you into a good man, not a good doctor, a good lawyer, or even a good philosopher, but a good man. So we can refine our definition of ethics as *the art of acting in such a way as to best achieve the ultimate purpose of human life*. With this in mind, let us begin.

CHAPTER 1

# The Meaning of Life

If someone were to ask you why are you doing what you are doing right now, what would you answer? ("Why," for example, "are you sitting in a classroom reading a philosophy book?") One student might say, "Because I like studying philosophy." Another might answer, "Because I have to be here." Still another might respond, "Because I want to get a good grade." All of these are proximate reasons for making choices, but they are not the ultimate reason why you are doing what you are doing. Let us take the example of the student who wants to get a good grade.

**Wise Teacher**: Why do you want good grades?
**Joe Student:** Because I want to get into a good college.
**Wise Teacher:** And why do you want to get into a good college?
**Joe Student:** To get a good job.
**Wise Teacher:** And why do you want to get a good job?
**Joe Student:** To make lots of money.
**Wise Teacher:** And why do you want to make lots of money?

**Joe Student:** [Feeling a little frustrated and thinking to himself, *Isn't it obvious why I want to make a bunch of money?! Everyone wants a bunch of money!*] Why do I want a bunch of money?! Because it gives me the freedom to do whatever I want!

**Wise Teacher:** And why do you want to be able to do whatever you want?

**Joe Student:** Because I want to be happy, okay!

**Wise Teacher:** Finally, we have reached the ultimate reason: happiness. Everything you do, you do because you want to be happy. And if you found out that making lots of money would not make you happy but rather unhappy, would you still choose to make a lot of money?

**Joe Student:** I guess not . . . but it *will* make me happy!

**Wise Teacher:** That remains to be seen. To know whether that is true or not, you have to know what happiness is. So can you tell me: What is happiness?

**Joe Student:** Ummm . . . [crickets] . . .

**Wise Teacher:** So you're telling me that the whole purpose of your life is to be happy, but you have no idea what happiness is? Doesn't that seem like a bad thing to you? What if I told you I was going to Lockport, but I had no idea where it is and no map that showed me how to get there, and I simply got up, went to my car, and started driving. Don't you think that would be foolish?

**Joe Student:** I guess it would be pretty foolish. So if I want to know how to become happy, then I will have to find out what happiness is first.

> **Wise Teacher:** That's right. And you can do that by trusting someone who already knows what happiness is and following his directions; or even better, you can discover for yourself what happiness is and then go there.

We can see from this dialogue that the first task of ethics is to define happiness, and not just with a nominal definition, so we know what the name means, but with a definition that corresponds to something in reality that can be the goal of our choices and actions. Like the definition of the soul, this will be a difficult task but one we can accomplish with some perseverance and careful thought. There is, perhaps, no more important and worthwhile definition you will ever find in your life than the definition of happiness, so it will be more than worth the effort!

As usual, it will be best to start with a nominal definition of happiness and move from there to an essential definition of happiness. Since it is human happiness we are looking for and not dog or fish happiness (if there are such things), the essential definition of happiness will be determined by the truth about what perfects and fulfills human nature. So we will have to make use not only of logic but also of the things we have learned in natural philosophy and the study of the soul.

## A Nominal Definition of Happiness

One nominal definition of happiness that we can start with is "that good for the sake of which everything else is chosen." Happiness is a good, and we choose every other good for its sake. So if we can find something that fits that description, we have found happiness. Another nominal definition of happiness is "the good that, by itself, totally satisfies all our desires."[6] If something makes us happy, then we do not need anything else. So happiness must be a good that suffices to fulfill our desires by itself. Using these two descriptions as a starting point, we can better hunt for happiness.

## Summary

- While there are many proximate reasons for our choices, there must be some ultimate reason, and we call this ultimate reason happiness.
- Since it is difficult or impossible to arrive at a destination without knowing where it is, and since happiness is the ultimate destination of our choices, it is most important in ethics that we discover a definition of happiness.
- There are many nominal definitions of happiness, including "that good for the sake of which everything else is chosen," and "the good that, by itself, totally satisfies all our desires."

[6] Sometimes it helps to have many nominal definitions of a thing to better understand it. Something similar happens in the five proofs for God's existence given by St. Thomas Aquinas, where five different nominal definitions of God are used, each one as the beginning of a demonstration.

CHAPTER 2

# What Happiness Is Not[7]

Sometimes, when looking for something very elusive, it is easier to find what you are looking for by first ruling out the places not to look. That seems to be the best way to start our hunt for happiness: determining what happiness is not. So let us round up some of the usual suspects and see if we can rule them out.

## Happiness Is Not Money

Money, at first, seems to be a good candidate for happiness. After all, almost everyone seems to want money, and the more, the better. That sounds a lot like happiness. But a little thought immediately shows that money cannot be happiness: money is

[7] Supplementary texts: Aristotle, *Nicomachean Ethics*, Bk. I, ch. 5; St. Thomas Aquinas, *Summa Theologiae* (hereafter STh.) I–IIae, q. 2; Book III of Boethius's *The Consolation of Philosophy*. NB: Mention should be made for how to read the references in the *Summa Theologiae*. There are three parts of the Summa, the First Part (Ia), the Second Part (II), and the Third Part (IIIa); the Second Part, however, has two parts, the First Part of the Second Part (referenced as I–IIae) and the Second Part of the Second Part (II–IIae). The next referential letter is "q," which stands for "Question;" however, each question has multiple articles within that one question, hence the "a," which follows the "q." Finally, each article has several components to it: the initial objections (referenced to as "obj."), the "on the contrary," which is the one line argument from authority (referenced as "s.c." [standing for the Latin *sed contra]*), the corpus (or body) of the argument (referenced as "c."), and the reply to the objections (referenced as "ad.").

only a means; it is never an end in itself. Happiness, however, is an ultimate end, not a means to something else. Therefore, money cannot be happiness.

It is obvious that money is only a means. What if someone gave you one hundred billion dollars on one condition: you (or anyone you gave it to) could not spend it or buy anything with it. Would you want one hundred billion dollars then? No, it would be more useless than dirt. The whole worth of money comes from what you can buy with it. It is also obvious that happiness is an ultimate end and not a means, since happiness is that for the sake of which everything else is chosen.

Not only that, but even as a means, money is very deficient: you cannot buy spiritual goods with money. You cannot buy love, or true friendship, or virtue, or wisdom. The Scriptures teach: "If a man offered for love all the wealth of his house, it would be utterly scorned" (Sg 8:7). True love is not the sort of thing that is for sale. At best, money can only be an instrument the good man uses to do good, as when he feeds the poor or builds churches for the worship of God, and so on. So once again, money is reduced to the status of a mere tool. It is not desirable in itself, nor is it self-sufficient, so it does not have the essential marks of happiness.

This explains why many people with a lot of money are so sad. It also explains why many of them are wicked. Sadness and wickedness are hardly compatible with the possession of happiness.

Look back now at the reasons people give for identifying the possession of money with happiness: all men desire happiness, and the more, the better. All men desire to have lots of money, and the more the better. Therefore, to have lots of money is happiness. Is there anything wrong with that syllogism (apart from the fact that the second premise is false)? Yes, it is an invalid second-figure syllogism. Notice how just a little logic can go a long way to help you avoid a wrong turn in seeking happiness!

## Material Goods Are Not Happiness

If money is not happiness, perhaps the things you can buy with money, e.g., houses, food, cars, vacations, are happiness. But if one thinks carefully about it, the same problems exist with these things as existed with money. Material goods are all somehow ordered to the goods of the body (for example, health, relaxation, physical comfort, or pleasure). Food is for the sake of health and pleasure, vacation is for the sake of relaxation, housing is for the sake of physical shelter and comfort, and even beautiful architecture or art or music is for the sake of pleasing the senses of sight or hearing. So material goods are all means to a further end. But happiness is not a means to a further end. Again, material goods are not sufficient to bring about spiritual goods like love, friendship, peace, virtue, or wisdom. So once again, we find that those who have an abundance of material goods are often sad and vicious and even tend to love their things more than other people, even their own family members.

## Happiness Is Not Power

If happiness is not money or material goods, maybe it is power. If someone has enough power, he can get whatever he wants, so that sounds like he would have all his desires fulfilled and, therefore, be happy.

But power cannot be happiness either. First of all, power can be possessed by the wicked. And it is not possible that the greatest good, namely happiness, could be possessed by one who is evil. For the greatest good should destroy all evil in someone, or else there could be a greater good than this supposed greatest good (namely, one that also removes the evil of wickedness). Secondly, no power could force someone to love contrary to his will. Hence, power will not be able to bring about a good that all admit belongs to happiness: love and friendship. Finally, power is a beginning of action, but happiness is not a beginning of any action but the ultimate end of all our actions. Hence, power cannot be happiness.

### Happiness Is Not Some Bodily Good

In general, most people tend to think that happiness consists of some bodily good like good emotions, sensible pleasure, or bodily health. Whatever is sought by all or most men in every time and culture is likely to be a good that belongs to human nature, so we cannot dismiss these physical goods: they must have some connection to happiness. I do not think you could say that a man is perfectly happy (at least as concerns natural happiness) if he is unhealthy, or in a lot of pain, or suffering from unpleasant emotions. Perfect happiness should completely fulfill or satisfy our desires, and clearly, we would have unfulfilled desires if these bodily goods were absent.

Nevertheless, happiness cannot *primarily* consist in some bodily good. Remember, it is human happiness we are seeking, not merely animal happiness. Animality is only part of human nature, but the best and most important part of our nature is the rational part. We naturally prefer our rational powers to our sense powers. No one, for example, would choose to keep his eyesight if it meant losing his mind. Even if someone were told that he could enjoy constant sensible pleasure, but only if he lost his mind, this would not be a good trade: your mind is what is, most of all, you. Without your mind, it would be as if someone else were enjoying that physical pleasure, but not you. This is why many people will even resist taking pain-reducing drugs when they are sick or dying since it reduces their capacity to think, to know, and to be aware.

From our study of the soul, we discovered an order in human nature: the goods of the body are ordained to the good of the soul. The soul is the substantial form and perfection of the body, and among the parts of the soul, the rational part is the most perfect and noble. Thus, for example, our imagination is for the sake of assisting our rational power to make inductions and abstract universals. This means that the goods of the body are not the ultimate end and so cannot be happiness. (Remember, happiness is that for the sake of which everything else is desired; it is not desired for anything else.) Not only that, but the goods of the body are all for the sake of preserving our substance in existence. But the ultimate end cannot be the mere existence of our substance. Everything that exists exists for the sake of some operation or activity beyond itself that constitutes its well-being. For example, the purpose of a knife is more than its mere existence: it is made to cut, and the purpose of an eye is to see, not just to be. Therefore, the goods of the body cannot be the ultimate end of man.

In summary, we can say that while bodily goods may be necessary to remove impediments to our happiness, and perhaps are even some part of natural happiness, they cannot be the most important or essential part of our happiness.

**Summary**

- Happiness is neither money nor found completely by having money.
- Happiness is not some external, material good.
- Happiness is not some good of our bodies (like health or sensible pleasure).
- Happiness is not power.

CHAPTER 3

# From a Nominal to an Essential Definition of Happiness[8]

## Happiness Is Some Good of the Soul

Now that we know that happiness is neither some material good outside of us nor some good of our body, we are in a better position to find happiness. Happiness seems to be something we experience within ourselves. This is true even if we admit that the experience of happiness might arise from the possession of something outside of us: the happiness itself is still something within us.

Not only that, happiness is only possible for things having knowledge. Rocks and trees are not happy. If we said they were, this would only be a metaphor. Even animals do not seem to be happy in the way that men are happy. Man seems to be capable of happiness in the full sense of the word. This is not surprising since man has a kind of knowledge that exceeds immediate sense knowledge, so that man can know being and goodness as such. This is implicit in our nominal definition of happiness: that good for the sake of which all other goods are chosen. Only man has free choice, so only man is able to choose among goods and perceive their order. Take the example of a man who falls in love

[8] Supplementary texts: *Nicomachean Ethics*, Bk. I, ch. 7; Bk. X, ch. 6–7.

with a woman and has that love reciprocated. Only because a man has universal knowledge is he able to promise and receive love for a lifetime and understand what that means. That makes possible a kind of happiness that sense knowledge cannot provide. So happiness must be some good of the kind of soul that is capable of knowledge, especially universal knowledge. In short, happiness must be a good of the rational soul.

### Is Happiness Found in One Thing or Many Things?

Granted that all men desire to be happy, is there just one thing that makes men happy, or are there many things? The *prima facie* evidence (the evidence from first appearances) inclines one to think that happiness is found in many things, not just one. After all, different men have different desires and values, and each seems to find joy and satisfaction in one thing or another, depending upon individual preferences. As the saying goes: "Different strokes for different folks." Again, man is a complex being, made of body and spirit. So for all human desires to be fulfilled, happiness would have to be composed of all the things that fulfill the various desires of human nature: sensible goods, spiritual goods, etc.

A complete answer to this question will have to wait until we have come to a more complete definition of happiness, but it is helpful here to point out a few reasons why happiness might be one thing rather than many. First, we share a common human nature with all men, and if happiness is the greatest good of man, it is what will, most of all, perfect human nature. Since human nature is one, happiness, the greatest good of human nature, will also be one.

The fact that not all men find satisfaction in the same things does not disprove that there is one happiness for all men since some people are better or more poorly disposed toward the goods that perfect their nature. For example, some people are healthy, and so they prefer healthy foods, while others are not healthy, and so they prefer unhealthy foods; yet this does not prevent healthy food from being good for all men, even if it doesn't *taste* good to all men. Therefore, the judgment of the one who is well disposed toward the good that perfects human nature should be preferred to the judgment of one who is not well disposed.

The fact that our nature is composite does not necessarily mean that the good that perfects our nature must also be composed. For while man is *potentially* many things, e.g., the human body has many organs, man is *actually* one thing, one substance. The various parts of man exist in him only as parts, not as actually existing wholes. Hence, if each part has a single purpose (even though it is something existing only in potency), then, for a much stronger reason, the whole man should have a single purpose since the whole man exists as actually one substance. Since this is the case, the good that perfects our nature ought to be a potential whole (instead of an integral whole), which has the power to perfect each part of our nature, just as white light has the power to illumine all of the colors. So there are good reasons for thinking that happiness is one thing and is found in one thing.

## An Inductive Argument for the Definition of Happiness

Now is a good time to begin a positive argument for what happiness *is* instead of what happiness is not. Going back to our nominal definitions of happiness, human happiness is man's greatest good: the good for the sake of which he chooses every other good. Happiness is also a self-sufficient good that satisfies all desires. The good of something is its purpose; it is what it is good for. For example, a knife is good for cutting, and that is also its purpose. Eyes are good for seeing, and that is also their purpose. But since happiness is the ultimate good of man, we are looking for the ultimate good, the ultimate purpose of man.

Finding the purpose of things is sometimes easy and sometimes difficult. If I were to ask you, "What's the purpose of a knife?" You would immediately say, "To cut." And if I were to ask you, "What's the purpose of an ear?" Again, you would know right away, "To hear." But as soon as I ask you, "What's the purpose of a man?" You draw a blank. It is difficult to identify the purpose of a man, so we should approach it through something easier to know.

It turns out that the purpose of a thing is also its proper activity, i.e., the activity that it alone can do or that it does best. We can manifest this inductively. What is the purpose of a knife? To cut. What is the proper activity of a knife? To cut. What is the purpose of a shovel? To dig. What is the proper activity of a shovel? To dig. What is the purpose of a pen? To write. What is the proper activity of a pen? To write. And in general, we can say that the purpose of any tool is its proper activity.

What is the purpose of an eye? To see. What is the proper activity of an eye? To see. What is the purpose of an ear? To hear. What is the proper activity of an ear? To hear. What is the purpose of a nose? To smell. What is the proper activity of a nose? To smell. And in general we can say that the purpose of any organ is the same as its proper activity.

What is the purpose of a teacher? To teach. What is the proper activity of a teacher? To teach. What is the purpose of a doctor? To heal. What is the proper activity of a doctor? To heal. What is the purpose of an architect? To design buildings. What is the proper activity of an architect? To design buildings. And, in general, we can say that the purpose of any profession is the same as its proper activity.

What is the purpose of the ability to play basketball? Actually playing basketball. What is the proper activity of the ability to play basketball? Actually playing basketball. What is the purpose of bravery? Brave actions. What is the proper activity of bravery? Brave actions. What is the purpose of free will? To act freely. What is the proper activity of free will? To act freely. And in general, we can say that the purpose of any habit or power is the same as its proper activity.

So, the purposes of a tool, of a bodily organ, of a profession, and of a habit or power are all the same as their proper activities. So, in general, we can see that the purpose of any thing is the same as its proper activity.

Now let us go back to the purpose of a man. It is not so hard to identify the proper activity of a man, so we can discover man's purpose by identifying man's proper activity. What is the activity that man alone can do, or the activity that he does best? To act according to reason. So man's purpose, his good, is to act according to reason. Notice, I did not say that man's proper activity is to reason but to act reasonably or according to reason. Man is not just reason, he is an animal with reason, so it is proper to man to act with reason, not just to reason. For example, playing ball with your son, singing a song, building a house, and doing geometry are all examples of acting reasonably. All of those activities in some way are man's purpose. This helps us to see the wide latitude of things that contribute to or constitute human happiness.

Looking back at our argument, we can form a series of syllogisms as follows:

Happiness is man's greatest good.
Man's greatest good is man's ultimate purpose.
Therefore, happiness is man's ultimate purpose.

Happiness is man's ultimate purpose.
Man's ultimate purpose is his proper activity.
Therefore, happiness is man's proper activity.

Happiness is man's proper activity.
Man's proper activity is to act reasonably.
Therefore, happiness is acting reasonably.

Man finds happiness in some degree whenever he acts in a reasonable way. Nevertheless, there are clearly some ways of acting reasonably that contribute more to happiness than others. Playing basketball is reasonable, but it does not compare to loving a friend, getting married, or begetting and raising a child. So, among reasonable activities, there is a kind of hierarchy we need to determine in order to find what reasonable activity, most of all, should be called happiness.

We can say generally that if happiness is reasonable activity, then the most perfect happiness will be the most perfect reasonable activity. But what makes one activity more perfect than another? An activity can be better than another for two reasons: either (1) it is about a better thing, or (2) it is done in a better way. For example, the activity of healing a man is better than the activity of healing a dog. (A sign of this is that we value the profession of doctor above the profession of veterinarian). This is because a man is better than a dog. On the other hand, one doctor might be better at healing a man than another. In this case, the activity is about the same thing, but one is better than the other because it is done in a better way. Another example: the activity of governing a country is better than the activity of governing a city. Hence, we honor the office of president more than that of mayor. But one president might govern the same country better than another, and one mayor might govern the same city better than another.

So there are these two ways in which one activity can be better than another.

It follows from this that the most perfect reasonable activity is the activity of reason done (1) with regard to the best object and (2) in the best way. Now, the best object of a reasonable activity would be the best thing that reason can reason about. But we proved in natural philosophy that the best thing is God. (Recall the fourth proof for God's existence where we proved that a greatest good that causes goodness in all other things exists).[9] Hence, the most perfect reasonable activity would be some reasonable activity that has God as its object. Moreover, the best way in which such an activity could be exercised is if the soul is well disposed for this activity by virtue: the wise and morally upright man is more able to contemplate God than the man who lacks wisdom or who desires to live contrary to the order God has established in creation.[10]

From these things, we are finally able to formulate an essential definition of happiness in the fullest sense: happiness is *the activity of contemplating God by means of virtue.*[11] In some way, this activity is that for the sake of which all other human activities are done. For if the body is for the sake of the soul, and the

---

[9] See STh., I, q. 2, a. 3, c.

[10] It is obvious that the wise man will reason about God in a better way, for he will have more certain and precise knowledge about God and will reason more easily with less error about God. It is also clear that the morally upright man will enjoy reasoning about God more than the man who lacks moral virtue. For the immoral man will experience guilt and shame when he reasons about God.

[11] Notice that this activity would primarily be an activity of the speculative intellect, which is the highest power of the human soul, so that the virtue primarily referred to here is wisdom. Also, remember that we are speaking of man on the *natural* level, not the *supernatural* level. The former is properly the question of philosophy; the latter properly belongs to theology.

lower powers of the soul are for the sake of the higher powers of the soul—for example, the vegetative is for the sake of the sentient, and the sentient is for the sake of the rational—and if the powers of the soul are perfected by their best activity, it follows that everything in man is for the sake of the best activity of the rational power.

## Another Road to Defining Happiness

We can come to the same definition of happiness by another road: the road of division from above. It is obvious that the name happiness corresponds to some existing thing. For if there were no ultimate reason for our choices, we would never choose anything. Just as there can be no infinite regress in efficient causes, so also there can be no infinite regress in final causes. For example, if I choose A only for the sake of getting B, and if I choose B only for the sake of getting C, then if C does not exist, there will be no reason for choosing A in the first place. For if I do not choose C, then I will also not choose B, and, therefore, I will not choose A. If the ultimate final cause is taken away, so are all the intermediate causes. So there must be an existing thing corresponding to our nominal definition of happiness.

Since happiness is an existing thing, in what category will it belong? First, it is clear that happiness is not a substance since a person can cease to be happy without ceasing to exist. Nor does a man change what he is simply speaking when he becomes happy or ceases to be happy: he remains a rational animal whether he is happy or not. So happiness must be an accident.

Among the accidents, happiness is predicated according to the mode of quality since it signifies how something is. Moreover, happiness has a contrary (misery); it allows of more and less, and one happiness seems to be like another happiness.[12]

The category of quality is divided into four species:

1. habit/disposition;
2. natural ability;
3. affective quality; and
4. shape.

But it is clear that happiness is not a shape, nor is it an affective quality since it is not the object of any sense, nor is it a natural ability since it is not merely an ability but something actual, and, unlike an inborn ability, it can be acquired. It follows, therefore, that happiness must fall under habit or disposition. Between these two, it is clear that happiness must be a habit and not merely a disposition since happiness must be something stable and long lasting if it is to be happiness. No one would call a good, which could be easily lost, the best good since it would be a much better good if it were possessed firmly and immutably. So happiness must be a kind of habit, in the sense of a firmly possessed quality.

Now a quality may be possessed as a first actuality or as a second actuality. In general, something can be actual in two ways: (1) it actually exists, and (2) it actually operates or performs some activity. For example, a horse actually exists (first actuality), and it actually runs (second actuality). This distinction not only applies to substances but also to other categories like quality. For example, someone can actually know something by having habitual knowledge of it (first actuality), or they can use or exercise

[12] Recall the three marks of quality from the categories.

their knowledge by actually thinking about what they habitually know (second actuality). Of the two, second actuality is more perfect since one who has second actuality also has first actuality, and since first actuality is for the sake of second actuality. For example, habitual knowledge is for the sake of actually knowing, and virtuous habits are for the sake of doing virtuous actions. Therefore, happiness must be a kind of quality that is an actuality or activity.

So far, so good. At this point, it will be helpful to call to mind that the name happiness signifies the complete satisfaction of desire. So what kind of activity completely satisfies desire? Since each thing has a natural inclination (i.e., natural desire) for its proper activity, it is clear that a thing's natural desire is satisfied by the performance of its proper activity [cue the orchestra to play the number from the musical *Show Boat* . . . "Fish gotta swim, birds gotta fly . . ."]. Moreover, this natural desire will not be *completely* satisfied unless the proper activity is done in the *best* way possible. So happiness will not be just any haphazard activity, but it will be the best proper activity of the one who is happy.

So far, we have the essence of happiness, but we still need the proper subject of happiness (just as last quarter, we found the essence of soul, "substantial form," but needed to find its proper subject, "natural, living body"). Well, where do we find happiness? Not in the body but rather in the soul,[13] and not just in any kind of soul but in a rational soul. Therefore, the definition of happiness with respect to its proper subject is the *best, proper activity of a rational soul.*

---

[13] In some way, happiness can be said to be in the composite of body and soul, though it is in the composite by reason of being in the soul, so happiness is said to be primarily in the soul.

From here, it is not too far to the definition we formulated above. For the nobility of an activity is determined by its object and its mode. And since the best object of rational activity is God, and the best mode of carrying out this activity is by means of virtue (especially the virtue of wisdom), it follows that the best proper activity of a rational soul is *the activity of a rational soul contemplating God by means of virtue, especially wisdom*. This definition is substantially the same as the one given above, except we have now reached it by way of division from more universal concepts rather than by means of induction.

The following chart will illustrate the progression in the definition with the left column indicating the elements of the definition and the right column indicating the experiences that lead to refining the definition with additional elements.

| **Elements of Definition** | **Experiences that Refine the Definition** |
|---|---|
| Happiness is the ultimate reason for choosing anything. (Nominal definition) | There is no infinite regress in causes. |
| Happiness is a real being. | To be happy is not to be. (A man continues to exist whether he is happy or not; put alternately, to be happy is not the same as to be.) |
| Happiness is an accident. | Happiness is predicated as that which makes something to be of such and such a sort: it indicates a way of being. |
| Happiness is a quality. | Happiness is not a shape, or an affective quality (since it is not the object of some sense power) or a natural ability (since it can be gained). Instead, happiness seems to be a state that is held in a stable way. |
| Happiness is a *habitus*.[14] | Second act (activity) is more perfect than first act.<br>Happiness is something most perfect. |
| Happiness is an activity. | Each thing has a natural inclination for its proper activity.<br>A natural inclination is *completely* satisfied when its proper activity is done in the *best* way. |
| Happiness is the best proper activity of a thing. | Happiness is primarily in the soul.<br>Happiness belongs most fully to rational beings. |
| Happiness is the best, proper activity of a rational soul. | |

[14] Here *habitus* does not signify a habit as opposed to an act but rather a stable having of some quality.

## Objective Happiness and Formal Happiness

At this point, it will be helpful to understand that we can speak of happiness in two ways. On the one hand, we can talk about the happiness that is the very activity we experience in our souls. This is sometimes called "formal" or "essential" happiness. On the other hand, we can talk about the object of this activity from which it derives its goodness: namely, God. Since God is the object of the activity in our souls, God is called "objective" happiness. The following text from St. Thomas describes this distinction:

> End is said in two ways. In one way the thing itself which we desire to obtain, just as money is the end of the avaricious man. In another way, the very acquisition or possession or use or enjoyment of the thing which is desired is the end, as when it is said that the possession of money is the end of the avaricious man and the enjoyment of a pleasurable thing is the end of the intemperate man. Therefore, in the first way the ultimate end of man is the uncreated good, namely God, who alone by His infinite goodness is able to perfectly fulfill the will of man. But in the second way, the ultimate end is something created existing in a man, which is nothing other than the acquisition, or enjoyment of the ultimate end...If, therefore, the beatitude of man is considered with respect to its cause or object, in this way it is something uncreated. But if it is considered with respect to the essence itself of beatitude, in this way it is something created.[15]

[15] STh., I–IIae, q. 3, a.1, c.

So, it is true to say that God is our happiness and the activity of contemplating God is our happiness (since we possess and enjoy God through contemplating Him). But of the two, God Himself is more perfectly our happiness since the goodness of contemplating God is caused by the fact that God is good in and of Himself.

### Happiness Consists in One Good

Now that we have a more precise account of happiness, we are in a better position to see why happiness is one good. When one good is desired for the sake of another good, the latter good is the reason for the goodness of the former good. For example, if the whole reason I want money is to buy something with it, then the thing I want to buy is the reason for the goodness of the money. Thus, the thing I want to buy is like a potential whole that includes the goodness of the money. Everything good about the money is contained in the thing I want to buy with it.

Similarly, all goods are ordered to the ultimate good and contained in that ultimate good as in a potential whole. For the goodness of everything we choose is for the sake of happiness, and nothing would be desirable at all apart from happiness. Even something as good as friendship would not be desired unless it made you happy. Therefore, happiness, the ultimate good, has the power to satisfy every human desire. God is just such a good since the goodness of all things is contained in God as in a first cause: God is the greatest good that causes all other things to be good. Hence, all the goods that man needs to satisfy his nature, bodily goods as well as spiritual goods, are all contained in God as in a potential whole. So happiness consists in one good.

## Summary

- The essential definition of happiness is *the activity of contemplating God by means of virtue (especially wisdom).*
- While contemplating God is not the only activity in which happiness is found (since all reasonable activity contributes to it), still the activity of contemplating God is like a potential whole that contains the happiness found in all other reasonable activities.
- Formal happiness is an activity of the soul, while objective happiness is the object of that activity, namely God.
- Happiness is one thing because human nature is one thing ordered to and perfected by one good.

CHAPTER 4

# Has Happiness Been Well Defined?

Here, a natural difficulty arises: if all men desire happiness, and if happiness is the activity of contemplating God by means of virtue, then it should follow that all men desire to contemplate God by means of virtue. But this is clearly false. Therefore, it seems that we have defined happiness badly.

In this syllogism, the term "desire" is used equivocally. In the one case, it means an inclination belonging to human nature, while in the other, it means a conscious act of the will. So, while it is true that all men have an inclination of their nature to contemplate God by means of virtue, it does not follow that all men will consciously choose this. The fact that most men do not consciously choose to contemplate God or strive for wisdom is not a sign that we have defined happiness incorrectly. Rather, it is a sign that men are, for the most part, badly disposed toward happiness, something verified by the sad fact that very few people seem to find lasting and authentic happiness. The case is much like that of a hospital in which very few people enjoy vigorous exercise, something naturally good and enjoyable to a healthy man but painful and difficult for a sick man. The fact that so many men are badly disposed to the contemplation of God and the acquisition of virtue is a confirmation of the truth of the doctrine of Original Sin.

## Perfect and Imperfect Happiness

There is, however, a more serious objection to our definition of happiness: happiness is supposed to satisfy all of our desires, but the activity of contemplating God by means of virtue will not satisfy all our desires. For example, we would still get hungry and tired and be subject to death. So, the activity of contemplating God by means of virtue is less than happiness should be.

If someone is hungry or dying or in any other pain, it is clear that they will not be able to contemplate God in the best way possible. So, contemplating God well implies or presupposes that these other goods will be present. Nevertheless, in this life, it is obvious that sorrow and death are unavoidable and that on account of fatigue, the contemplation of God would be, at best, intermittent. And even if someone is not presently subject to any suffering, still the fact remains that he knows he will die, and so his happiness will not be all that it should be, and something will be left to desire. But the defect is not so much in the definition itself as in the fact that the reality signified by this definition is not possible in this life.

Aristotle recognized this fact and concluded that perfect happiness is not possible in this life, so a man should try to achieve the closest approximation to it that he can: a kind of imperfect but humanly possible happiness. Such an approximation would be a full life lived according to virtue for the sake of the contemplation of the best things, especially God. This approximation is the best that the philosopher can point to as a goal in human action. The fact that man has a natural desire for a happiness that is greater than that possible in this life suggests that there must be the possibility of perfect happiness after this life. This brings us back to something we observed at the very beginning of our course on philosophy. Besides the order produced by reason and discovered by reason, there could also be an order revealed to reason. Such an order revealed to reason by God would be necessary if man is to prepare for perfect happiness after this life.

## The Beatific Vision

Philosophy is an account of the ultimate causes of reality *according to human reason*. As such, philosophy does not pretend to give an account of the whole picture, an exhaustive explanation of all reality, but only the part of reality accessible to human reason. And one thing human reason sees is that its perspective is limited and incomplete. For example, human reason sees that soul and body are naturally united in man but also that there is no natural cause that can reunite soul and body after death so that the human soul has no natural way of escaping an everlasting, unnatural state. Again, human reason sees that there is a natural desire for perfect happiness but also that there is no natural way to achieve perfect happiness. These philosophical difficulties need an answer that philosophy cannot provide. Yet, revelation does provide an answer to these questions.

According to revelation, God brings about a resurrection of the body so that soul and body do not remain forever in an unnatural state. And according to revelation, God makes perfect happiness possible after this life. This happiness consists in the direct, unmediated vision of the divine essence. That is to say, according to revelation, by God's help, man can know what God is in Himself, not merely through His effects. This direct knowledge of what God is is called the beatific vision since it makes those who see it perfectly happy or beatified.

How does the beatific vision compare to our philosophical definition of happiness? Our definition of happiness was the activity of contemplating God by means of virtue. The beatific vision is also an activity of contemplating God, but instead of contemplating God by means of some human virtue like wisdom, God is contemplated by a divine virtue or power granted to the soul. This divine mode of contemplating God is a much better way of contemplating God than human virtue, so the beatific vision especially corresponds to our conception of happiness as the activity of contemplating God in the most perfect way possible. The revealed truth about human happiness perfects and completes what we discovered about happiness from reason unaided by faith. As St. Thomas Aquinas teaches, "Grace does not destroy nature but perfects it."[16]

The nature of the beatific vision and the means to prepare for it is the subject of theology, a higher science than philosophy. So we must set it aside for now. As philosophers, we see that the acquisition of virtue is the necessary means to achieve human happiness in this life, so we now turn to a consideration of virtue. But to begin, we must ask: What exactly is virtue?

### Summary

- The fact that few men consciously and actually desire to contemplate God is not a sign that happiness does not consist in the activity of contemplating God but rather a sign that most men are badly disposed to in their souls: something confirmed by the fact that so few find happiness.
- The happiness knowable through reason is an imperfect form of happiness, and we have a natural desire for something more perfect.

[16] STh., I. 8, ad. 2. Supplementary text: R. McInerny, *A First Glance at St. Thomas Aquinas*, ch. 20, "Aristotle and the Beatific Vision."

- The revealed truth about the beatific vision harmonizes with and perfects our definition of happiness.
- The doctrine of Christ about the beatific vision gives an account of how the perfect happiness we naturally desire can be attained.

CHAPTER 5

# Virtue: The Road to Happiness

If happiness is the destination sought in all our choices, then virtue is the road along which we must travel to arrive at happiness. Just as a destination cannot be reached if there is no road or path open to that destination, so also happiness cannot be reached without virtue. Without virtue, man is not sufficiently free to choose the activities that result in happiness. Virtue expands our freedom, giving reason free rein to operate to its maximal abilities, while vice contracts our freedom, making reason a slave to disordered emotions or bad habits. A simple example will help illustrate: if I have never played the piano in my life or have never taken any piano lessons, I simply am not free to play a Mozart piano concerto since I do not have the ability to do it. I need a certain amount of excellence in piano playing before I am free to play a complex and beautiful piece.

Or again, unless I have built up my strength by frequently lifting lighter weights well, I will not be able to lift a heavier weight like two hundred pounds. I am not free from the beginning to lift two hundred pounds until I have built up enough strength (which is like a virtue of my body). Similarly, unless my moral life and intellectual life are strengthened by virtue, I will not be free to choose the best things, and the contemplation of God will be, at best, laborious and difficult. This kind of freedom can be called the freedom of virtue or excellence since, by acquiring certain virtues, our freedom is expanded to embrace the best things. The saint is free to know and love God in ways that the average person cannot even imagine. Freedom of virtue should be contrasted with freedom of potentiality. This kind of freedom is what the beginning piano player has: he can pound the keys as he pleases but, without the habit of piano playing, he cannot choose to produce anything of great beauty. So freedom of potentiality is less perfect than freedom of virtue.

In this chapter, we shall first consider the definition of virtue; second, identify the main kinds of virtue; and last, describe how these virtues can be acquired, strengthened, and preserved.

## The Definition of Virtue

As Plato suggested in his dialogue the *Meno*, it is easier to begin with examples of virtues than with a definition of virtue. Justice, temperance, fortitude, prudence, wisdom, etc., are all kinds of virtues. So to define virtue, we will have to determine what all of them have in common.

Let us begin by examining each of the ten categories to find the genus of virtue. It is easy to see that virtue is not a substance. And it is easy to see that virtue is not a quantity or an outfit, or a position, or a where, or a when, or an acting upon, or an undergoing.

So that leaves two categories: quality and relation (toward another). At first, it might seem that virtue is somehow toward another. We speak of a virtue *of* the soul and a virtue *of* courage. Aristotle even gave examples of virtues in his chapter on "toward another" in the categories. But recall the distinction Aristotle made between names that are relative according to the way we speak about them (*secundum dici*) or according to their very being (*secundum esse*). Virtue is not relative or toward another in its very nature, like right and left, or double and half, since I can think about virtue without thinking about something relative to it. It is true that virtue has an opposite (vice), but vice is opposed to virtue as a contrary, not as a correlative, since vice is not in the very definition of virtue, and since it is possible that virtue could exist without vice existing. So that leaves quality. Qualities allow of more or less, and so does virtue. Qualities have contraries, and so does virtue. Qualities are said to be similar or dissimilar, and so is virtue, as when one man's virtue is said to be like another man's virtue, or when clemency and mercy are said to be similar virtues. In this example, mercy is the virtue that dispels the misery of another,[17] while clemency is the virtue that mitigates punishment.[18] So virtue seems to fall clearly within the category of quality.

Recall that there are four species of quality: habit (or disposition), natural ability, affective quality, and shape. Among the species of quality, virtue is clearly in the species of habit since it is a lasting disposition of the soul that can be acquired. So we can say that the genus of the definition of virtue is "habit." This agrees with our examples of virtue: justice is a habit of giving to each person what they deserve; temperance is a habit of suppressing concupiscence; fortitude is a habit of overcoming fear; wisdom is a habit of judging the highest truths; and so forth.

But how is virtue distinguished from vice since both are habits? Simply put, virtue is a good habit that perfects its possessor and makes his actions good, while vice is a bad habit that is a defect

17 STh., II–IIae, q. 30, a. 1, c.: "As Augustine says (*De Civ. Dei*, ix, 5), mercy is heartfelt sympathy for another's distress, impelling us to succor him if we can. For mercy takes its name *misericordia* from denoting a man's compassionate heart [*miserum cor*] for another's unhappiness."

18 STh., II–II, q. 157, a. 1, c.: "Clemency 'is leniency of a superior in inflicting punishment on an inferior,' as Seneca states (*De Clementia*, ii, 3)."

in the one who has it and makes his actions bad. So virtue is a good habit of acting.

It is also clear that virtue is a habit in or of *the rational soul.* Virtue does not belong to inanimate things, nor even to mere animals, but to men. And it is not in the human body that virtue resides but in the part by which a man lives and acts in a rational way. There is no virtue of growing well or of keen eyesight. These are perfections but not virtues.

So, in summary, we can give an initial, broad definition of virtue as *a good habit of acting in a rational soul.*

## Moral and Intellectual Virtues

As we learned in the study of the soul (volume III), the rational soul has an appetitive part and a knowing part. Not surprisingly, there are virtues for each part or power of the rational soul. The virtues of the appetitive part are called the moral virtues, while the virtues of the intellectual (knowing) part are called the intellectual virtues.

In the rational soul, some parts are able to be influenced by reason, while others are not. For example, the vegetative part of the soul cannot be influenced by reason.[19] On the other hand, the rational appetite, also called the will, is rational in itself. Somewhat between the vegetative power and will stands the sense appetite. While we cannot simply decide to feel one way or another, the sense appetite can be influenced and even trained by reason to respond to certain events in a certain way, as when we choose to act according to or against the way we feel. Recall that the sense appetite includes the concupiscible and irascible appetites.[20]

---

[19] See Matthew 6:27: "Which of you by being anxious can add one cubit to his span of life?"

[20] Refer back to chapter 11 of volume III of this series, *The Study of the Soul.*

Whenever a power of the soul is able to be influenced by reason, it is possible for a virtue to reside in that power of the soul.

## Moral Virtues

Moral virtues are those that make a man desire what is right and act well. Hence, moral virtue is a perfection of the appetitive (or desiring) part of the soul. To have virtue in its fullest sense, it is necessary not only to want what is right but to choose to do what is right. Choice is the act that completes our desire.[21] Thus, moral virtue is a habit of *choosing* well. Choosing well in moral matters means choosing between two extremes. For example, the temperate man chooses between too much food and too little food. The brave man chooses between confronting too much danger and too little. But notice that this mean between extremes is usually not exactly in the middle: often, it is closer to one of the extremes. Most men have a much greater tendency to eat too much than to eat too little. Most men have a tendency to flee in the face of too small a danger. So the mean is usually not exactly halfway between the extremes: it is established by right reason. Not only that, but each individual will have a different mean. For example, the right amount of food for a little girl is different from the right amount of food for a grown man. So how do we determine the mean? By the judgment of what is *reasonable* in the given circumstances.

Take the example of temperance: reason sees that the purpose of food is nutrition. Therefore, normally, the right amount of food is the amount of food that will provide sufficient nutrition for a given individual to perform his duties well. Too much food

---

[21] Once we have deliberated about the various means to the end we desire and determine our appetite to one of these means by a choice, the act of the appetite is complete, and all that remains is to carry out the choice by our actions.

will result in lethargy in the short term and excess body fat and health problems in the long term. Too little food will result in fatigue and compromised health or even starvation. But even this is subject to particular circumstances. Say that you have eaten enough food, and you feel satisfied, but there is cake for dessert. Normally, the right thing to do is not to eat the cake. But if it is your wedding day, and it is customary for the bride and groom to eat the wedding cake, the right thing to do is to eat the cake, even when you feel full. So practicing virtue demands prudence. If we put all of these factors together, we can define moral virtue as *a habit of choosing in the mean, according to reason and relative to us, as the prudent man would do.*

### Intellectual Virtues

Virtue can also reside in the knowing part of the rational soul. The rational soul has both a practical knowing power (practical reason) and a speculative knowing power (speculative reason). The practical reason is the part that puts order into things, while the speculative reason is the part that discovers order in things. Recall that the end or purpose of a practical knowledge is making or doing something (think of recipes in a cookbook or numbers in a phone book), while the end of speculative knowledge is knowing the truth itself. There are intellectual virtues for both the speculative and practical reason.

### Art and Prudence

Since practical truths are ordered to making or doing something, there is a virtue for making things, called *art,* and a virtue for doing things, called *prudence*. Examples of art include the habitual knowledge by which someone builds houses well or grows crops well, the various martial arts by which someone has the knowledge of fighting well, and even the fine arts, such as painting, sculpture, and music. The example I gave earlier of someone playing a Mozart concerto was an example of someone acquiring the virtue of the art of piano playing. Art can be defined as *right reason about things to be made*, or even more distinctly, *a fixed and definite procedure established by reason by which human acts reach their due ends through appropriate means.* The perfection of art is found in the thing made: a bad man can still make a good table or even a good piece of music.

In contrast to art, the perfection produced by prudence is found in the prudent person himself. Prudence is a knowledge that directs our own actions and choices in such a way that we can effectively find the means to happiness for ourselves and for others. Prudence can be defined as *right reason about the things to be done*, or even more distinctly as *a habit of choosing the appropriate means to a due end as determined by reason*. Thus, the perfection of prudence is found in the act that a person does; it is a perfection of the person himself. Hence, a bad man might be cunning, but he cannot be prudent. Prudence is directive of the moral virtues as implied in the definition of moral virtue. Without prudence, the moral virtues cannot exist in their perfection.

The knowledge that you are acquiring while studying ethics contributes to prudence, for ethics sets down the principles of good action. But the knowledge provided by the study of ethics is not sufficient to make someone prudent. The knowledge acquired by studying ethics is too universal to be a sufficient principle of right conduct. Every human act is particular and individual. Therefore, in addition to universal principles, there is also needed particular experiences and habits by which a man knows the best course of action in the here and now, the very particular circumstances that inevitably accompany every real choice.[22] A man who has raised several children has experiences (sometimes by trial and error) that the man with no children does not have. So the man who has raised many children is often in a better position to know what to do in this or that circumstance in order to bring about a good result in the moral life of a child. The best way to learn prudence is to seek in docility the advice of older persons who have successfully directed their own lives and the lives of others to happiness.

Because of its close connection to the moral virtues, prudence is sometimes considered to be a moral virtue. Yet, it must be recognized that prudence is not called moral in the same sense that the other moral virtues are called moral: the other moral virtues are perfections of the appetite, while prudence is a perfection of a knowing power.

## Understanding, Science, and Wisdom

The speculative reason also has virtues. This is obvious from experience. There are some people who, from acquired habit, reason better than others, who make fewer mistakes, and who are more accurate and precise in their knowledge. The virtues of the speculative power of reason differ from those of practical reason in that speculative reason is ordered to knowing truth for its own sake, while practical reason seeks to know only for making or doing things. For example, to know whether there is a greatest prime number is not for the sake of making or doing anything but simply to know something about the nature of number. And we

[22] St. Thomas Aquinas points out that prudence straddles two powers of the soul: the practical reason and the sense powers. Prudence begins in reason but ends in the senses (specifically, the cogitative power of the soul). See STh., II–IIae, q. 47, a. 2–3 (specifically a. 2, c. & a. 3, ad. 3).

do not seek to know if each angel is its own species for the sake of making or doing anything with that knowledge.

There are three virtues that perfect the powers of speculative reason: understanding, science (or "reasoned-out" knowledge), and wisdom. This can be manifested as follows: since the end of the speculative reason is truth, and since all perfectly known truths are either self-evident or demonstrated, there is a virtue about coming to know the first self-evident truths and a virtue about coming to know truths acquired through demonstration. The virtue about coming to know the first self-evident truths is called *understanding* and can be defined as *the virtue of the mind by which the immediate and universal statements are firmly grasped.* The virtue about coming to know truths through demonstration is called *science* and can be defined as *the virtue of the mind by which the universal and necessary conclusions drawn from first, immediate statements are firmly grasped.* These two virtues are especially developed through the art of logic. Besides these two intellectual virtues, there is a third intellectual virtue called *wisdom,* which is the highest perfection of the speculative intellect. Once the virtues of understanding and science have been acquired, the mind is able to look back upon the whole body of knowledge and perceive the underlying order and ultimate causes of all truths. Thus, wisdom can be defined as *the virtue of the mind by which one grasps the first and most universal causes of things and by which one judges all science and understanding.* Wisdom is developed through the acquisition of all the sciences but especially through the speculative sciences that deal with the most universal causes: natural philosophy and metaphysics.

## The Need to Follow a Guide on the Road to Happiness

The general sketch I have given about happiness and virtue might leave the reader with the impression that attaining happiness is just about getting a good definition of happiness and a good definition of virtue and then setting about acquiring the various virtues by repeated acts. But the truth of the matter is that there is another essential ingredient to becoming happy: a guide, both in the moral life and in the intellectual life, i.e., a teacher.

There are at least two reasons for this. The first reason is that we naturally receive our first formation from others in both the moral and intellectual life. Our reason has very little control over our emotions when we are young, and so it is not able to rightly form them. Besides this, when we are young, reason is incapable of forming itself or its own acts. Little children live by faith in what they are told. This state of affairs is inescapable as a byproduct of human nature that begins in a state of radical imperfection.

The second reason is that even after we have acquired the ability to regulate our emotions and form our own reason, there is still a great difficulty in arriving at perfection in the moral or intellectual life. To discover the right path to virtue and truth involves so much trial and error and such a vast array of experiences that no single individual could advance a significant way by himself toward perfect moral or intellectual virtue. Individual human choices involve a virtually unlimited number of possible circumstances, and so much trial and error are involved in hitting the precise target that it is practically impossible to become perfectly prudent without learning from the experiences, successes, and failures of others. The same is true in the life of the mind. As one of my former teachers once said to me, "I read Newton's *Principia* and learned in three hours what I could not have discovered on my own in a million years!"

And so, perhaps the single most important element in successfully acquiring virtue and becoming happy is having a wise and prudent guide to lead you along the way. Trying to become happy without an experienced guide is like trying to scale Mount Everest without an experienced guide: practically speaking, it is impossible. Perhaps it was this fact that caused Aristotle to rewrite his first treatise on ethics and to rename it the *Nicomachean Ethics*, thus greatly honoring his own father and first teacher, Nicomachus.

## The Passions of the Soul

Since many of the moral virtues concern the sense appetite, it will be helpful to sketch an outline of the various emotions or passions of the soul by which the sense appetite is moved. The word "passion" is derived from the Latin *passio*, which simply means an undergoing (like the category opposed to acting upon). So the soul is acted upon by some object and undergoes something like a movement or motion (hence the English word "emotion"). This undergoing or motion in the soul is not exactly the same as a physical motion in a material subject, but there is enough of a likeness that the same name is used in an analogous sense. Recall from our study of the soul that the activities in the soul are determined and defined by their objects. So the various passions of the soul, which are kinds of activities, will be differentiated from one another by their respective objects.

The fundamental object of any appetite is some good. This good can be considered simply, without any further qualification, in which case the passion that is the response to any sensible good is called *love*[23]; or this good can be considered as absent, in which

[23] The emotion of love should not be confused with the love that is an act of the will. The former has a sensible good as its object, while the latter has a good perceived by reason as its object. In fact, many of the emotions have the same or similar names as corresponding acts of the will. Here, we will restrict ourselves only to emotions in the strict sense: movements of the sense appetite in response to a sensible object.

case the passion that arises is called *desire*; or this good can be considered as present, in which case the passion that arises is *joy*.

Not only is the sense appetite inclined toward good, but it is also inclined away from the contrary of good: evil. Hence, in response to sensible objects perceived as evil, there are three other passions that arise. In response to a sensible evil taken simply, the passion of *hatred* arises. In response to an absent sensible evil, the passion is *aversion*, while the response to a present sensible evil is called *sorrow*. These six emotions: love, hatred, desire, aversion, joy, and sorrow are the emotions of the concupiscible appetite.[24]

There are five other emotions found in the irascible appetite. Recall that the irascible appetite is that power that has as its object some good or evil with a special difficulty associated with it. This difficulty is not just a matter of degree; it is of such a nature that it requires a formally distinct act of apprehension to determine whether or not it is in one's power to obtain the good or avoid the evil. The dog, seeing the rabbit at a distance, needs to consider further whether or not it is in his power to catch the rabbit.

When a difficult good is considered to be possible to obtain, the passion that arises is *hope*, while if it is considered impossible to obtain, the passion that arises is *despair*. On the other hand, when an evil that is difficult to avoid is considered possible to overcome or avoid, then the passion that arises is *daring*, while if it is considered impossible to avoid or overcome, the passion that arises is called *fear*. The last passion of the irascible appetite is *anger*, from which the irascible appetite takes its name (from the Latin *ira* meaning "anger"), probably because it is the most noticeable emotion of the irascible appetite. Anger arises when a

---

[24] The word "concupiscible" comes from the Latin word *concupiscere*, which means "to ardently desire." This implies that, of the emotions found in the concupiscible appetite, desire is the best known.

past evil (hence impossible to avoid) is considered as possible to avenge. There is no contrary emotion for the good, though the closest would be something like gratitude, the response one feels for a good received that is possible to somehow repay.

Notice that there is a certain order among these passions of the soul. In particular, love has a certain primacy over all the other passions since all the passions that have a sensible good as their object presuppose love. This is because any perceived good, whether present or absent, easy or difficult, will, first of all, be loved insofar as it is good. And since good is primary in relation to evil (evil is defined as the lack of a good that ought to be in something), love also has primacy over the passions that have an evil object. Therefore, unless something is loved, none of the other passions will be present. To take an example, if some sensible good is absent and difficult but possible to obtain, the person will first experience love (as soon as he perceives it as good), then desire (as soon as he perceives it as absent), and then hope (as soon as he perceives it as possible). So at the same time, a person could experience love, desire, and hope. Hope is like a potential whole that includes both desire and love.

The following tables will be a convenient reference for laying out the eleven passions of the soul. The first table lays out the passions of the concupiscible appetite, while the second table lays out the passions of the irascible appetite.

| | Good | Evil |
|---|---|---|
| Simply | *love* | *hatred* |
| Absent | *desire* | *aversion* |
| Present | *joy* | *sorrow* |

| | Good Difficult to Obtain | Evil Difficult to Avoid |
|---|---|---|
| Possible | *hope* | *daring* |
| Impossible | *despair* | *fear* |
| | *anger* (impossible to avoid but possible to avenge) | |

We noted above that these passions are able to be influenced and even trained by reason, but they can also influence one another. The passions are naturally subject to reason, so they are perfected and developed when reason intervenes to curb an unruly passion, as for example, when a man sees that it is unreasonable to have sexual desire for a woman who is another man's wife. However, the passions are not naturally subject to one another, so when one passion overrides another passion contrary to reason, this is called repression and can be harmful to a person's emotional life. For example, a man might have such a fear of lust that his emotion of fear represses even reasonable sexual desires, such as those between a husband and his wife. Repressed emotions eventually resist the repressing emotion, and often this results in an overwhelming experience of the repressed emotion that completely binds reason. Therefore, it is important that young people learn to train their passions by reason rather than by other emotions.

## The Cardinal Moral Virtues

Now that we have briefly considered the passions of the soul, we are in a better position to examine the cardinal moral virtues: temperance, fortitude, justice, and prudence. The English word "cardinal" is derived from the Latin word meaning "hinge," like the hinge upon which a door hangs. So these virtues are called cardinal virtues because they are the hinges upon which the other virtues depend and a central focus around which other virtues are grouped.

## Temperance

The virtue of temperance can be defined as the habit of choosing the reasonable mean in regard to *physical pleasures*, especially those dealing with the sense of touch and taste, such as pleasures associated with reproduction and nutrition. These physical pleasures especially arouse the passion of desire, so that temperance is particularly concerned with moderating this passion.

The excess vice with regard to pleasures of nutrition is called gluttony, while the defect has no common name since it is so rare. The temperate man eats that quantity and quality of food that is sufficient for nutrition and bodily health. Bodily health is the reasonable mean or target at which reason aims because reason sees that eating and drinking are for the sake of the existence and health of the body. The glutton misses the mark, usually by excess quantity, but also by foods of bad quality (e.g., candy), and by being more concerned about the preparation of his food than is reasonable. The defective vice almost always involves eating either too little or foods that are too plain to provide proper variety in nutrition. Gluttony is much further from temperance than the defect, so in order to acquire temperance, one ought to aim more toward the defect than the excess. In other words, the temperate man eats less than most men feel is enough.

The excess vice with regard to the pleasures associated with reproduction is called lust, while the defect is not well known (since so few people have it) but could be called insensibility. The temperate man chooses to use his reproductive power when it is reasonable to reproduce and in a manner that is ordered to reproduction. Since it is obvious that children are best raised and educated when both the father and mother cooperate and are in a lifelong, loving union, it is clear that the reproductive power should be used only within marriage.[25] And since the reproductive power ought to be used in a manner that is ordered to reproduction, it follows that anything that in itself takes away the possibility of reproduction during the reproductive act is unreasonable. Thus, contraception is unreasonable, as is using the reproductive organs in such a way that they cannot work together to bring about reproduction. But using the reproductive organs in such a way that they each perform their complementary functions yet do not result in conception because of temporary or long-term infertility is not unreasonable. For the organs have been used the way they are intended to be used but themselves have a material defect. It is completely different to use good organs in a bad way and to use bad organs in a good way. So contraception and natural family planning (having marital relations during periods of infertility) are completely different. Lust is much further from the mean than insensibility, so when aiming for temperance in this area, one should aim farther away from lust.

### Fortitude

The virtue of fortitude (bravery) can be defined as the habit of choosing the reasonable mean with regard to *fearful things*. And while there are many fearful things, such as snakes, spiders, and dentists, nevertheless, the virtue of fortitude is determined by the greatest among fearful things. And since the most fearful thing is death, fortitude is especially found in confronting the fears concerning death. But recall that fortitude is a habit *of choosing*,

[25] Marriage is defined as a lifelong union between a freely consenting man and woman for the sake of the procreation and education of children.

and that implies that not just any danger of death is the matter with which fortitude deals but the kind of danger of death that can be chosen or avoided. For example, the fear associated with the dangers of combat or with the danger of speaking against the evil actions of a tyrant who could kill you are the kinds of fears that fortitude deals with most of all. However, right conduct in facing any kind of fearful thing in some way contributes to fortitude. The desire for physical pleasures is something that tends toward excess in most men, but it is the opposite with fear of danger since most men are less inclined to confront those dangers than they should be. So while temperance moderates and holds back a passion that is inclined to excess, fortitude bolsters and fortifies a passion that is inclined to defect.

The excess of fortitude is recklessness and is found when a man unreasonably exposes himself to dangers. Such persons are thrill seekers but are not truly brave since they are not afraid of things they should fear, nor do they seek some reasonable good through confronting these dangers. The defect of fortitude is cowardice and is found when a man refuses to confront or expose himself to a danger when he ought to. For example, when a man does not defend his wife against an attacker, or when a soldier flees rather than defends his country, he is responding to his fear in an unreasonable way. Fortitude is not halfway between recklessness and cowardice but is closer to recklessness than to cowardice. This is why the reckless man is sometimes confused with the brave man, while the coward never is. But insofar as both recklessness and cowardice respond to fear in an unreasonable way, fortitude is unlike both: it is not so much between these vices as above them.

Someone might think that it is never reasonable to expose oneself to death for any reason since when someone ceases to exist, he loses every good. One way to respond to this objection is to point out that there is an afterlife in which rewards or punishments will be given by God. True as this is, it is not entirely knowable from reason alone. It takes some faith to see this. From reason alone, we know that the human soul endures after death, but we know very little about its condition or about its relationship with God. After all, God is a free agent, and how He chooses to interact with us after death is up to His free choice. So when Aristotle confronts this problem, he simply points out that the person experiences more good and more happiness in the brief moment in which he exposes himself to death than he would have in an entire lifetime pursuing mediocre goods and living with the shame of having been a coward.[26] So we see that while faith is a great aid in developing fortitude, still, even without faith, one can see that it is better to undergo death than to do wrong or fail to do what one ought.

### Justice

Justice is the habit by which one chooses to give to each person what is due to him. Unlike fortitude and temperance, justice is a habit in the will (the rational appetite) rather than a habit formed in the sense appetite. Hence, justice is nobler than temperance or fortitude and pertains more to the common good than they do.

Because there are two fundamental kinds of communication among men, there are two species of justice. The first kind of communication is when one person exchanges goods with another person, and the justice concerned with this kind of communication is called commutative justice. The second kind of communication is when someone distributes goods to a number

[26] Homer seems to make a similar point in his epics *The Iliad and The Odyssey*, in which both Achilles and Odysseus are given the choice between living forever with a mediocre life or living a heroic life that will end in death.

of persons (for example, when the executor of a will distributes the goods of an estate to its heirs). The justice concerned with this kind of communication is called distributive justice.

In commutative justice, strict equality is the rule. If I give you five pairs of shoes, and you give me one suit, this exchange will be just if the worth of the five pairs of shoes is equal to the worth of the suit. But if, for example, the shoes are much higher quality and took much more labor and skill to make than the suit, the exchange will be unequal and, therefore, unjust. Usually, the factors that go into determining the objective worth of some physical good are time and intensity of labor, the skill of the one who makes it, and the nobility of the product itself (for example, a medical device that is ordered to the production of health is more noble than a cooking utensil that is ordered to the production of food). However, there may also be other factors involved, depending on the circumstances. Besides physical products, there are also services that can be exchanged for physical products or other services. For example, a lawyer puts his knowledge of law at the service of one who wishes to understand and make better use of the law, and a doctor puts his knowledge of medicine at the service of one who wishes to be restored to health, and a teacher puts his knowledge at the service of one who wishes to obtain a good education.

In distributive justice, the rule is proportional equality. For example, if a man gives ten percent of the initial capital for a company, then he deserves to receive ten percent of the profit from that company in return. Again, if one player on a team contributes more to the victory than the others, then he is due greater honor than the others. Thus, there is equality of proportion since the honor given to each member is in proportion to the contribution each one made to the victory.

### Acquiring Virtues: Repeated Choices and Actions

Now that we have examined some of the principal intellectual and moral virtues, it is important to see how such virtues are acquired and strengthened. Typically, a habit will not be acquired or lost by a single action. It requires many repeated actions to acquire a habit firmly. Think of how much time must be spent at the piano to acquire the habit of playing the piano well. It is similar with the virtues.

To acquire a certain virtue, it is necessary to make choices repeatedly and carry out the actions that are like the choices and actions of a virtuous man. To form the virtue more quickly and perfectly, the choices and actions should be performed at or near the maximum intensity of which one is capable. To take an analogy, if someone wants to develop strong muscles, he will have to lift weights regularly that are at or near the maximum weight he can lift. The more he does this, the stronger he becomes, and his maximum weight increases as time goes on. It is similar with virtue. The man who repeatedly and reasonably confronts as great a danger as he is capable of confronting grows in the virtue of fortitude. The man who repeatedly and reasonably resists the inclination to eat too much food grows in the virtue of temperance.

Finally, with virtue as with bodily strength, unless you use it, you lose it. Virtue is not only lost through contrary actions, such as unjust or intemperate actions, but also through habitual neglect to use the virtues you already possess. True, vicious actions will destroy virtue more quickly, but inaction and negligence in using virtues will just as surely destroy those virtues over time. To preserve acquired virtues, it is necessary to regularly use those virtues at or near their maximum ability.

Of course, all this presupposes that our choices are such as would be chosen by a virtuous man. The good man is the measure of moral virtue, and the wise man is the measure of intellectual virtue. In order for someone to grow in these virtues, it is normally necessary that they have the example and counsel of one who already possesses the virtue to some degree.

**The Principles of Ethics Are Often Taken from Habituation**

Every science and every art (including ethics) proceeds from principles that are self-evident. For example, the geometrician begins from the principle that the whole is greater than the part and that when equal quantities are added to equal quantities, the sums are themselves equal. Some self-evident first principles are obvious even to persons with very little experience. It is obvious that the same thing cannot be and not be in the same way. It is obvious that motion exists. It is obvious that living things are different from non-living things. Such self-evident truths are acquired without much reflection or effort. It is as if they find us rather than us finding them. However, many of the first, self-evident principles of ethics are not discovered that way. The first principles of ethics tend to be acquired through habituation to certain acts. Hence, these principles are not obvious to everyone but only to those who have habitually acted in a certain way or who have had experience with these moral realities. This is why ethics is more easily acquired by those who are older (though it can still be of some profit to the young as well). Below is a list that gives examples of some of these principles. These are only a few examples and in no way are intended to be an exhaustive list.

- Repeated actions produce inclinations for those actions.
- Resisting anger in a reasonable way over a long time reduces its force.

- Resisting sexual desires in a reasonable way over a long time reduces their force.
- Fasting habitually reduces sexual desires.
- Spiritual pleasures are more delightful than bodily pleasures.
- Spiritual pleasures grow the more often they are repeated.
- Bodily pleasures diminish the more often they are repeated.

Some of these principles are well-known even to young people. For example, a young person has enough experience with bodily pleasures that he is aware that bodily pleasures tend to diminish as they are repeated. Food eventually becomes repugnant to the man who eats and eats and eats. On the other hand, it is likely that many of these principles do not seem obviously true to you. Some may seem only probable, while others may even seem counterintuitive. For example, resisting anger or sexual desires seems like it would cause a buildup of pent-up emotions and, finally, an outburst. This might happen in the case of a repressed emotion, but so long as the emotions are resisted in a reasonable way, this will not happen. Instead, the emotions will grow more and more calm. But this is only obvious to someone who has habitually disciplined his emotions in this way.

Someone may object that this makes ethics subjective, but, in fact, it does not. These principles are still objectively true since everyone who habituates himself in this way finds out that they are true. This underscores the importance of having a good moral example in ethics. A good man is the one you ask about how to act so that you will acquire virtue. Ethics is not a matter of plugging numbers into a formula; it involves following someone along a path who has already found the way.

## Summary

- Virtue is a good habit of acting in a rational soul.
- Virtues can be moral or intellectual
- Moral virtue is a habit of choosing in the mean, relative to us, and according to reason, as the prudent man would choose.
- There are eleven passions of the soul that are distinguished according to their objects.
- Virtues are acquired by repeated actions at or near one's maximum ability.
- Some of the principles of ethics are evident only from habituation.

CHAPTER 6

# Choice and Human Acts

Since moral virtue includes choice in its definition, and since virtue is acquired through repeated good choices, it is essential that we briefly consider choice as well as that which causes a choice to be good or bad before we move on to the topic of virtue.

## Voluntary Actions

Choices are *voluntary human acts*. It is important to distinguish a properly *human act* from an *act of a human*. It can happen that a human being performs some action but without the intervention of reason or deliberation. For example, when a man walks down the street, he may unknowingly kick a leaf on the ground. Or again, a man struck on the funny bone may extend his hand. Digestion, blood circulation, and sweating also occur without human deliberation. These are acts of a man, but they are not properly called human acts since an act of a human is *an act that happens* ***without*** *the mediation of that which makes a man to be a man (reason).* A human act, then, is *an act that has its origin in reason, that which makes a man be a man.*

In short, a human act is done deliberately by reason, while an act of a human occurs without reason's specific, deliberate command. A human act is proper to human beings alone, while an act of a human is oftentimes found done in beings with sensitive souls.

A *human act* is said to be voluntary when:

1. it proceeds from an intrinsic principle and
2. from knowledge.

If a man grabs your hand and, by force, uses it to pull the trigger of a gun, then that act was not voluntary since the source of the action was external to you. On the other hand, rocks fall downward on account of an intrinsic principle but have no knowledge, so their acts are not called voluntary. Both need to be present for an act to be voluntary.

### Choice

Since every agent acts for an end, this will be true also of voluntary agents. In fact, acting for an end seems to be especially obvious in voluntary agents. Whenever a voluntary agent acts, it is with a view to some good (real or, at least, apparent). For example, a man decides to go to New York because he thinks he can make a good business deal there. Now typically, once some good is desired, there are several possible means to arrive at that good. For example, one way to get to New York is by car, another by train, and another by airplane, and often many airplanes leave and arrive at different times. So before acting, a man needs to limit himself to one of these possible means.

So, in most human actions, there is the apprehension of the good desired and an apprehension of the means to that good. Then there is a kind of deliberation in which the agent decides what is the best means (taking into account the various circumstances) for him to get that good. Finally, the agent determines himself the one means that is immediately within his power to do. This is the moment of choice. Choice is this determination of the one means as the conclusion of a deliberation. Choice is an act of the will that is the result of deliberation by the reason, so both will and reason cooperate in every choice.

## Making Good Choices: Object, End, and Circumstances[27]

In order for a human act to be good, it must be able to lead the one who performs it to happiness. One way to understand sin (a bad human act) is as an act that cannot make the one who does it happy. So avoiding sin is not primarily about breaking some arbitrary rule or law. Avoiding sin is essential for happiness. Conversely, performing good acts is essential for happiness.

Human acts can be understood in a way that is analogous to natural substances. For a natural substance to be good, three things have to be present:

1. a natural substance must have some definite species (e.g., it must be a horse or a parrot or some such thing);

2. a natural substance must have the accidents that perfect it (e.g., a horse should have all four legs, and a parrot must have wings); and

3. a natural substance must have a right relation to its final cause (e.g., an eye must be well disposed for seeing since seeing is the end or purpose of an eye).

[27] For a more complete treatment of the principles by which a good or bad choice can be determined, consider chapters 2–3 of *Understanding Marriage and Family: A Catholic Perspective* (Waterloo, ON: Arouca Press, 2020). I wrote this work as an apologetics primer for high school students on these two topics: marriage and the family. This work can be used as a supplementary text to this chapter.

Analogously to whether or not a natural substance is good, three things are necessary to make a human act good (i.e., able to lead to happiness):

1. the object of the act must be good;
2. the circumstances of the act must be good; and
3. the end or intention of the act must be good.

Unless all three of these—the object, the circumstances, and the end—are good, the act will not be good since a defect in anything essential results in the whole being evil. Just as a horse that does not have even one of its legs is a bad horse, and an eye that can do everything but see is a bad eye, so also a human act that does not have a good object, intention, or circumstance is a bad human act.

Universally speaking, we can say that the **object** of an act is *that which the act is about or that upon which the act bears*. This is the most fundamental element needed to make an act good. The object makes the act be the kind of act it is (for example, the object of seeing is color, and color makes seeing the kind of act it is).[28] The object answers the question of "What is done?"

The **circumstances** are *the accidents that "stand around" the act but do not make the act to be the kind of act it is*. For example, singing is an act, and *loudly* is a circumstance of the singing; singing more or less loudly does not make singing to be what it is. However, if the circumstances have some reasonable or unreasonable relationship to the act, they can alter the moral evaluation we make of that act.

---

[28] An act that has an evil object is what we call an "intrinsically evil act"—the act itself necessarily is evil, despite the best intentions and the best circumstances. Some examples of this are murder (the intentional killing of the innocent) or blasphemy—there can never be any intention or circumstance that ever permits or justifies either of these two acts (see CCC 1756, 1761).

The **end** or intention is *that for the sake of which the agent acts* (or that for the sake of which the act is done). This answers the question of "Why is it done?"

Examples will be helpful here, so the following are several examples of human acts in which I will identify the object, circumstances, and end and will also evaluate whether the act is good or not.

***Example 1: A man eats a steak.***

Take a simple human act: a man eats a steak. Let us evaluate the moral quality of this act. The steak is the object of the act of eating. In itself, that is okay since a steak is the sort of thing that can be digested by the nutritive power of man. On the other hand, if instead of eating a steak, the man decided to eat steel wool, there would be a disorder here since reason sees that the human nutritive power is not capable of assimilating steel wool. Let us say the intention of the man in eating the steak is for nutrition. That is also good since reason sees that eating is for the sake of nutrition. But let us say instead that the intention of the man is not nutrition but rather mere pleasure or even because he wants his little brother to go hungry, so he even eats the steak when he is not hungry himself. This would be a bad intention. Let us say the circumstances are that he is at home sitting down to dinner with his family. Those are good circumstances in which to eat a steak. But what if, instead, he is sitting in a chapel during Mass. Those are not good circumstances in which to eat a steak since it would be disrespectful and distracting to himself and others.

***Example 2: A man chooses to drive his car to work while drunk so he can support his family.***

Here, the object of the choice is the act of driving a car.[29] In itself, this is a reasonable thing to do, so there is nothing wrong with the object. The end or intention is to support his family. That is good and reasonable too. So far, so good. But then, when we look at the circumstances, we see that driving while drunk is unreasonable since it is likely to result in harm or injury to others or oneself. So, even though two of the factors are good, the whole act is bad since the third factor is bad. Overall, he has made a bad choice.

***Example 3: A husband chooses to have intercourse with his wife in their bedroom only for the sake of pleasure while using contraception.***

Here, the object of the choice is a reproductive act that is carried out in such a way as to render reproduction impossible. Notice that the object of his choice is not simply a reproductive act but an impeded reproductive act: impeding reproduction is part of what he chooses to do. Reason sees that reproductive organs are for the sake of reproduction, so when they are used in a way that frustrates their purpose, this is unreasonable. So the object here is bad. The circumstances are both good since it is reasonable to carry out a reproductive act with one's wife in one's bedroom. The end is bad, however, since to carry out a reproductive act *merely* for the sake of pleasure is disordered. The pleasure is not bad in itself, but it is insufficient as a reason for engaging in a reproductive act with another person: the good of the other person should also be intended, and the possibility of offspring should not be positively

---

[29] Notice here that the object of the choice is itself an action, where the object of the action of eating in the previous example was a thing (a steak). So the object of a human act can be either a thing or another action. Since choice is an internal act of the soul, the object of choice will always be some other action.

excluded from one's intention since this is the natural purpose of the act itself.[30] So, since at least one of the factors is bad, the whole choice is bad.

***Example 4: A man chooses to have intercourse with his wife for the sake of showing her love and affection while she happens to be infertile.***

Here, the object of the choice is a reproductive act. This object is in itself good since the propagation of the human race is good. The circumstances are that the woman is his wife (good) and that she happens to be infertile. The infertility, while itself a defect in her reproductive power, is not a circumstance that makes the choice bad since the reproductive act is not itself altered in such a way as to impede reproduction. Remember, it is completely different to use a reproductive organ badly than to use a bad reproductive organ. The defect in the reproductive organ is not something intentionally caused. So this circumstance is not morally bad, nor does it render the choice morally bad. The end is good since it is reasonable to show love and affection to one's own wife in this way. In addition, if the man desires a child to come from the act, even though he realizes it is unlikely, this end is also good and reasonable. So, since the three factors are good (or at least not bad), the whole choice is good.

Hopefully, these examples will help to clarify what is meant by the terms "object," "circumstance," and "end." In every human act, each one of these is vital in determining an action's goodness or lack thereof.

## The Principle of Double Effect

It sometimes happens that some human acts involve something unavoidably bad, a physical evil, yet it is clear that these human

---

30 See *Humanae Vitae*, 12, 14, 17.

acts with mixed results ought to be done nonetheless. But first, we must be clear: this is absolutely not a case of the object, end, or circumstances of the act being evil in themselves. If that were true, the whole act would be bad. This foundation for all of morality excluding a bad object, a bad intention, or bad circumstances from all good acts still applies—evil means are never justified by a good end. Rather, this is a case of an evil that is foreseen as an *effect* of the act but is not intended as *part* of the act. To determine whether or not one should choose to do an act where there is a foreseen evil, the principle of double effect[31] must be applied. At the end of the day, the principle of double effect is not adding more but is simply making more clear what is already inherently contained in the rules for the three sources of morality.

The conditions of the principle of double effect are as follows:

1. a good must be intended;
2. the foreseen evil must not be intended either as a means or as an end;
3. the good intended cannot be caused by the evil;
4. the good intended must outweigh or at least be of equal weight as the foreseen evil; and
5. if multiple means can equally accomplish the good, then the one with the least foreseen evil should be chosen.

We see that these conditions ensure that the sources of a human act—the object, circumstances, and end—are all good. Conditions 1

[31] This principle of moral decision making is called "double effect" since it is foreseen that the act will have both an intended good and an unintended evil effect.

and 2 must be present for the end or intention to be good. Condition 3 must be present for the object to be good. And conditions 4 and 5 must be present for the circumstances to be good.

Let us take an example to help clarify. A pregnant woman has a cancerous uterus that cannot be treated without killing the baby and which will certainly result in the woman's death if it is not treated. If she has the uterus removed, is that a morally good choice?

Is there a good intended? Yes, the saving of her life. Is the foreseen evil intended as a means or as an end? No. She does not intend the death of her baby as an end. Indeed, she wills the opposite. Nor is the death of the baby willed as a means or as an end, such as a substitute for an abortion. The means she intends here is the removal of the cancerous uterus that happens to result in the death of the baby. Is the evil the cause of the good? No, since the death of the baby in no way causes her improvement of health; rather, it is the removal of the cancerous uterus that causes her restoration to health. Is the good of greater or equal weight as the foreseen evil? Yes, since each life is taken to be of equal value. Moreover, if it is certain that the baby would have died anyway, it is better that one life be saved instead of losing both, that is to say, that only the baby die than that both the mother and baby die. So overall, this can be a morally good choice. If there is a good chance that the baby could live if the uterus is not removed right away, then it would also be a good choice for the mother to sacrifice her own life so that her baby could live. Indeed, it would be a better choice, though either choice would be morally acceptable.

On the other hand, if a woman were to have an abortion in which the life of the baby was directly taken, this would not be a good choice. For then, the evil would be the cause of the good, and the evil would be intended as a means to the good. So both the intention and object would be evil in such a scenario. Therefore, a direct abortion is always morally wrong since it always involves intentionally taking an innocent life.

This concludes our consideration of the principles for determining what makes a moral act to be good or bad. These principles apply in all cases and have no exceptions. Yet, while the student should appreciate once again that while these principles are what allow him to determine the good and the bad, it will often be necessary to take counsel with a good and prudent man in more difficult cases where the application of such principles is unclear or difficult. Wisdom is gained by experience, and ethical principles, while vital, can never do away with the need to consult the prudent man, as prudence guides all the other virtues. Universals can be difficult to apply to particulars. This is why the virtue of prudence is so necessary for moral conduct: "Prudence is the knowledge of what to seek and what to avoid."[32]

## Summary

- A voluntary act is one done from an intrinsic principle and with knowledge.
- Choice is a voluntary act determining the will to some means within our power as the conclusion of a deliberation.
- For a human act to be good, the object, circumstances, and end of that act must all be good.
- When doing some good involves a foreseen evil, the principle of double effect can be used to evaluate whether or not that moral act is good.

[32] STh., II–IIae, q. 43, a. 1, s.c.

CHAPTER 7

# Natural Law[33]

The ability of human reason to discover the purposes for natural things and the order among natural things gives rise to a kind of naturally discoverable moral code that serves as a rule for human action. When a man comes to understand human nature and the things that perfect human nature, he immediately appreciates the fact that the things that perfect human nature ought to be done and the things that are opposed to the perfection of human nature ought to be avoided. This appreciation of what ought to be done or avoided can be expressed in practical statements, such as "do good and avoid evil," "love your children," and "do not harm the innocent." These practical statements and others like them are an expression of what is called *natural law*. A man sees that unless he acts according to these practical statements, he will not and cannot be happy.

Here, it will be helpful to give a definition of law and to explain how a law can be "natural." Law, in its rudimentary sense, is a rule or measure of human acts. Just as a ruler is set against a board to see if it is straight, so too a law is considered together with a human action to see if it is upright. More precisely, law

33 STh., I–IIae, q. 91, a. 2. Supplementary texts: R. McInerny, *A First Glance at St. Thomas Aquinas*, ch. 18–19. Also see *Understanding Marriage and Family: A Catholic Perspective*, ch. 2.

is an ordinance produced by reason for the common good of a community, which is made and promulgated by the one who has care of that community.[34] This is the definition of what is commonly called man-made law or *positive law*. Some examples of these laws are "do not pass through an intersection when the light is red" and "do not steal an automobile." The word *law* is also used to name other practical directives that are not made by any particular human ruler for a particular society. Human reason, even unaided by faith, can discover that in order for human nature to exist and flourish, human beings must follow certain practical statements or directives. We call these statements expressions of a *natural law*, as if human nature itself is giving us precepts to do some actions and avoid others. For example, "care for your children" and "do not kill the innocent" are statements of this kind. Obviously, the word *law* is being used here in a different but related sense to the definition of law given above: law is not used univocally when we speak about man-made law and natural law, but it is used equivocally for a reason.[35] Nevertheless, because of the close likeness of the practical directives of the natural law to the practical directives of man-made laws, there is good reason to use the word law for both.[36]

---

[34] STh., I–IIae, q. 90, a. 4.

[35] Recall words used univocally, words used equivocally by reason, and words used equivocally by chance discussed in the logic text (volume 1), chapter 7.

[36] Once it has been discovered by philosophy that there is a divine being who has instituted the order in the universe and human nature in particular, these practical statements can be seen as a kind of participation of the directives that God intends for mankind to observe. In this way, the likeness between positive law and natural law becomes more apparent, since there is a divine lawgiver who has care of the community and who promulgates this law by writing it upon human hearts. The directives in the mind of God that he wants us to obey are sometimes called the *eternal law*. Ultimately, therefore, natural law can be seen as man's participation in the eternal law.

To avoid confusion, it should be understood that this natural law is not the same as what physicists call ***the laws of nature***. The laws of nature—such as the law of gravity or the third law of thermodynamics—are descriptive accounts of how non-rational things actually behave. The natural law we are considering here is not just a description of what actually happens but rather ***the expression of what ought to be done or chosen by a rational being***. A rational being may choose to act contrary to the natural law (and he is blameworthy for doing so), while a natural thing has no choice but to behave as described by the laws of physics. So, natural law is not the same thing as the laws of nature or physics.

As we have already seen, natural law is also not the same as positive law. Positive law is *a law that is the result of convention or agreement or someone's decision, not a law that results from the very nature of things*. Traffic laws are a good example of positive law. There is no reason in nature why someone should stop at a red light and go at a green light. It could be just the opposite. But those who govern our country have established that stopping at a red light and going at a green light is the convention we should follow.

All just positive law is ultimately based upon and a determination of some natural law. For example, the statement "do not harm the innocent" is a precept of the natural law. But the precept that "the penalty for assault and battery is a minimum of one year in prison" is a precept of positive law, giving some determinate penalty for one who violates that natural law precept. Positive law is always supposed to facilitate the keeping of the natural law. Even a law like "stop on red and go on green" is ultimately for the sake of facilitating some natural law precept such as "men should cooperate together in a way that avoids harm to their persons and damage to their property."

Natural law is universal to human nature and does not change from society to society. It is just as wrong to kill the innocent in New York as it is in Antarctica. Anyone who consults his reason rightly can see what ought to be done and avoided in the most fundamental cases. These fundamental cases are the first principles of the natural law and are obvious to anyone who has the use of reason and does not have a corrupt will. The most fundamental of all natural laws is "do good and avoid evil." As this precept is applied to more and more particular instances, it becomes harder and harder for reason to see what ought to be done and avoided. For example, it is easy to see that one should honor his parents since they are causes of his coming into existence, but it is not always easy to see what specific signs of honor ought to be given to them. Again, it is easy to see that one should not lie and that one should not harm his neighbor, but what if lying seems to be the best way to avoid harming your neighbor? This shows the necessity of consulting a good and prudent man to determine how best to follow the more specific precepts of the natural law. It also shows how important it is for those who make positive laws to be prudent and good. Otherwise, they may frame laws that are contrary to the natural law.

Just because positive law is not natural law and can change from society to society, this does not mean that persons in that society are free to disregard positive law. In fact, it is a precept of the natural law that men should obey just positive laws. For it is necessary, if men are going to live together, that they be subject to a common authority and live by the same laws. Imagine if everyone decided to disregard the law that you should stop at a red light simply because it is not a natural law. Many people would be injured or killed, and society as a whole would be greatly harmed. Similarly, when a society establishes a minimum drinking age, all those who are members of this society are morally bound to obey this law, even if they are not likely to abuse alcohol. It is sinful for a person to simply excuse himself from obeying the just positive law because he thinks he is the exception to the rule. This attitude ultimately means that each person gets to make the laws for himself, which is destructive of society. No one wants to live in a society where people think that they can excuse themselves from any law they want.

It may happen that some societies are so morally corrupt that positive laws do not reflect or are even opposed to natural law. In some societies, murder, theft, self-mutilation, adultery, fornication, and other unnatural sexual acts are permitted or protected by law. Such laws are only laws in name, but they are not morally binding. Sometimes, a man is morally bound to act contrary to such corrupt positive laws, as when a man rescues the innocent from death, even though this is against the law.

Earlier, we proved the existence of an all-good, all-wise God who governs the universe. (Recall especially the fourth and fifth proofs for God's existence.) This means that the natural order is established by this all-wise Creator and reflects His wisdom. Hence, in its most profound sense, natural law can be seen as a participation in the eternal order that God has established in creation. Natural law is simply man sharing in God's plan for governing the universe.

### Man Is Naturally Social

When we consider the goods of human life, we can see that some can be obtained by an individual more or less by himself, like basic food, clothing, and shelter. Others can be obtained with the help of a family, like friendship, children, and a basic education. Others can only be obtained within a society working together, like an advanced education, peace and security from dangers, artwork, well-made homes, etc. As a general rule, the better goods can only be acquired within a larger community since they are the result of common action. Therefore, the best use of human freedom requires that we act together in union with other persons, for that freedom is greater that makes it possible for us to obtain the better goods. For example, a young man who marries gives up a lesser freedom (e.g., the ability to spend leisure time with his friends late at night) for the sake of a greater freedom (the ability to beget and raise his own children). From this, we see that social life is important for the flourishing of human freedom. Hence, it is part of the natural law that man live together with others, both in a family and in some larger community called civil society. Man is naturally a social animal.

## The Family[37]

A family is *a communion (a multitude of people living a common life together) composed of a husband, a wife, and their children.* A married couple without children is not a family but a couple. The special name beyond "couple" comes from the new community formed by the parents and children. And the right definition is "husband and wife," not "father and mother," because a true family requires marriage (whereas having children does not). The marriage is part of the cause of the stability and unity of the family.

In this definition, we can see the four causes (form, matter, agent, and end) implied. "Communion" is the form since it states

---

[37] The treatment of family ethics here is necessarily cursory. For a brief treatment of the Church's official teaching on the family, consult CCC 2201–2233. For a fuller treatment of domestic society (marriage and family) see the aforementioned *Understanding Marriage and Family: A Catholic Perspective*, which addresses this very topic more deeply and specifically for a high school audience.

what family is. This form implies the end or purpose of family life: living a common life together. A communion is more than a mere community since it implies a shared life, not just a multitude united by a common goal. "Composed of" signifies the parts or matter: "husband, wife, and their children." The husband and wife, by their free consent, are also, in some sense, the agent causes producing the family.

Someone might ask if this definition is too restrictive. After all, we consider grandparents, aunts, uncles, cousins, etc., to be members of our family. But these relationships are more remote, and we would typically call them our "extended family." What is defined above is the "nuclear family," which is the first community formed, and the larger ones arise out of a multitude of marriages and such families. For example, the reason our grandparents are part of our family is because they are related to our parents.

It is obvious that the family, as defined above, is natural. In his *Politics*, Aristotle gives one of his famous sayings: "Man is by nature a political animal."[38] That is, man seeks to live in a community in virtue of being a man, and the first community is the family. Man cannot even come into existence and receive basic nourishment without being cared for in a family. Also, the basic foundations of moral and intellectual education are found in a family. So both man's being and well-being naturally depend upon a family. Moreover, marriage is natural, and family is the natural result of marriage; therefore, family must also be natural.

Like any other community, the family depends on and exists for the sake of certain common goods. Each child is a common good to every other member of the family. The other children who await a new baby will gain a new person with whom they will

[38] *Politics*, 1253a.

share a common origin and with whom they will live a common life. Clearly, too, each parent is a common good of each other person in the family. Not only is each parent, taken singly, a good for all the other members of the family, but also the marriage between the husband and wife is good for each of them and for each of the children. (Consult children who have gone through awful divorces.) The child naturally loves his mother and father since he is like a combination of them, and so when they fight and hate each other, it is like he is being torn apart. The harmony between all the members of the family is also a common good of the family. Domestic peace makes possible domestic happiness—a life of common activities that are a common joy and perfection to each of the members of the family.

These are some of the most important common goods shared by the members of a family. When these goods are cherished and promoted, family life is happy and healthy.

### Civil Society

It is obvious that a singular family, by itself, is not capable of fully perfecting a man. An isolated family might be able to provide basic food and shelter and the basics of education, but many perfections, including a profound education in the arts and sciences, are not possible merely within one isolated family. There must, therefore, be a larger community of which man is naturally a member. Aristotle again argues that this is something that is a part of human nature: "The impulse to form a partnership of [a city-state] is present in all men by nature."[39] We can see why men have this "impulse" because doing so allows man to perfect himself.

---

[39] *Politics*, 1253a.

The "most complete," or "perfect," human community is that political community that has everything needed to actualize or fulfill man's highest natural abilities. If it did not possess these things, either there would be some other community that does possess them, and then this other community would be more perfect (and from this, it would follow that there was something more perfect than the most perfect), or no community would possess the things necessary for actualizing man's highest natural abilities, and thus nature would have endowed man with these abilities in vain. Since neither of these options is admissible, it follows that the most perfect human community is that political community that has everything needed to actualize or fulfill man's highest natural abilities.

Such a perfect community would not only provide the bare necessities needed for generation and survival but also those things necessary for man to live a perfect life according to reason and virtue. "The end of law and of a regime is not to dishearten [men], but to make men virtuous: and this is the end of politics."[40] This is because that which is specific to and highest in human nature is reason. The perfection of man demands that the potencies of a rational nature be actualized to the highest possible degree, but for this to take place, it is necessary that all of those human faculties ordained to the perfect exercise of reason be actualized.

When a political community is sufficiently large and well organized so as to provide the conditions and incentives necessary so that a life of reason and virtue can flourish among its citizens, then such a community is a most perfect human community.[41] To

---

[40] St. Thomas Aquinas, *Commentary on the Psalms* 44, n. 5.

[41] Among the organizations necessary for such a perfect community to exist would be, for example, educational institutions where human wisdom can be pursued in an orderly manner.

the degree that a political community is deficient in these areas, it lacks the notion of a perfect community.[42]

From these considerations, it is clear that men are naturally perfected by and naturally members of both a family and a civic society.[43]

### The Relationship Between Family and Civil Society

Some think that since political life is also natural to man and is even a more principal end—a more perfect community—that those who have authority over the whole community can also alter the nature of marriage and family as they see fit. Notice that it is not true that the larger and more complete community can simply absorb or replace or restructure the smaller and more partial one as it sees fit—not any more than a community can absorb the individual.

It would not be natural for man to live in a community at all or to be social if the community somehow replaced or destroyed his individual activity, e.g., doing all his thinking for him and making all his decisions for him. In that case, social life would be destructive of the individual, not perfective of it.

Similarly, it would not be natural for a family to live in a community with other families if the larger community thus formed replaced the families so that the whole was like one big

---

[42] Of course, this is not to be understood as a kind of utopian civilization where, in fact, every person is provided with all the means necessary to achieve personal fulfillment. It suffices that a political community have all those civil organs that are indispensable for the acquisition of the moral and intellectual virtues, even if, for a given person, or in a given case, the circumstances necessary for full human development are lacking. Needless to say, if a political community is to have the notion of a perfect community, it must be possible for at least some (and, ideally, as many as possible) of its citizens to arrive at the perfection of moral and intellectual virtue.

[43] Supplementary text: Appendix B (*Civic and Family Life*).

family, and parents no longer had authority over their children, but only the clan chief or tribal lord had authority over children. Such an arrangement would destroy the family, not perfect and fulfill it.

Family life is not merely a means to certain good results but is itself an end and a fulfillment of human desire. Therefore, even when those in charge of some more complete community can do certain things more effectively than the parents of a family can do them for themselves, it is in many cases better to let the parents do them, and wrong (and contrary to nature) for the civil authorities to usurp these powers to themselves.

This completes our consideration of natural law and the societies in which man is naturally a member. Since man is naturally social, we should also consider friendship. Indeed, the greater part of happiness seems to be found in friendship.

## Summary

- Natural Law is the rule of human action that reason discovers by understanding the natural purposes and order among things.
- Because of man's inability to achieve perfection by himself, man is naturally a member of a larger society.
- In particular, man is naturally a member of both a family and civil society.
- The family cannot be simply absorbed or replaced by civil society.

CHAPTER 8

# Friendship[44]

In his *Nicomachean Ethics*, Aristotle devotes two entire books to friendship, and other than happiness, it is the topic he considers in the greatest detail. So it is clear that, for Aristotle, friendship was one of the most important elements of the happy life. In introducing the topic of friendship, Aristotle says that friendship seems to be a virtue or something above virtue. It is an undeniable fact that friendship is one of the greatest goods of life. No virtuous man would choose to live without friends. St. Thomas ultimately describes friendship as a kind of property flowing from virtue and virtuous living, as if to say no one can live virtuously without making and living with friends.[45] Aristotle observes that a friend is "another self," and for that reason, friends "double our joys

[44] There are masterpieces on friendship every person would benefit from reading. Aristotle's *Nichomachean Ethics* devotes two entire books to this topic, so vital is understanding friendship for living out an ethical life. The student who reads books 8–9 of the *Nichomachean Ethics* would invest his time well. Additionally, Cicero's stand-alone treatise *On Friendship* is well worth the read. Aelred of Rievaulx's work *Spiritual Friendship* is revered as a classic, and commentaries by the Fathers of the Church on Christ's Last Discourse (John 15) are helpful in this matter. For present day literature, C.S. Lewis's *The Four Loves* devotes its fourth chapter to friendship.

[45] It was said about St. Thomas Aquinas that he was so faithful a friend that after his death the members of his community could not speak of him without shedding tears.

and halve our sorrows," which then makes friends "the greatest of external goods." Religious traditions, including Judaism and Christianity, clearly teach the importance of friendship for the moral life. The Book of Sirach spends many verses extolling the merits of friendship.[46] In the New Testament, Jesus said, "Greater love has no man than this, that a man lay down his life for his friends" (Jn 15:13). It is evident, therefore, that the virtuous man ought to have friends and that the consideration of friendship belongs to ethics.

The connection between friendship and happiness is obvious even to young people, who largely tie their sense of well-being to good friends. Nor is this simply a phase through which young people pass. Even in the mature stages of life, and even among the wise and most virtuous, friendship seems to be essentially connected with happiness. So it is clear that any treatise on ethics must consider friendship and the way in which friendship contributes to happiness.

## The Definition of Friendship

What is friendship? It is remarkable how something so common in human life can be so difficult to define. One thing is clear: friendship involves love. So Aristotle recommends looking at the ways things are lovable. Sometimes we love something merely to be used by us, as a man might love a good bottle of wine. But it is not like that with friendship: a person loves his friend *for his friend's sake*. And yet, his friend is also *his* good. These

[46] Sirach 6:14–17: "A faithful friend is a strong defense and he that has found him has found a treasure. Nothing can be compared to a faithful friend, and no weight of gold and silver is able to countervail the goodness of his fidelity. A faithful friend is the medicine of life and immortality: and they that fear the Lord, shall find him. He that feareth God, shall likewise have good friendship: because according to him shall his friend be."

two statements may seem incompatible: How can someone love something for himself and yet for the sake of another? To see how this is possible, it must be understood that what is for you is not always for your sake. Being a citizen of a just country is good for you, even if your country does not exist for your sake, i.e., the whole good of the country is not ordered to you as to its ultimate end. If that were the case, you would be no different than a tyrant who required that all the citizens in a country serve his private good. What is good *for* you is perfective of your nature and contributes to your happiness. What is good *for your sake* is ordered to you as to its ultimate end or purpose. In the same way, a friend is good for you, something perfective of your nature that contributes to your happiness, and yet he is not loved for your sake, but rather he is loved for his own sake.

The fact that a friend is your good and loved for his own sake implies that you share a common good together. A common good is able to be shared by many at the same time without being diminished. This good is your good and your friend's good. By loving this common good, it becomes your good. By willing this good to belong to your friend, you love your friend for his sake, that he, like you, might enjoy this good. When both you and your friend are united in love of this common good, there arises a union of wills and affection. Therefore, friendship is a union of wills and affection between persons.

Not just any common interest or union of wills makes for friendship. Two people may share the same profession or hold the same truths, but this does not necessarily make them friends. Friends are united by a common good that they both share and love together and in each other.[47] So every friendship requires that

47 C.S. Lewis notes: "Friendship arises out of mere Companionship when two or more of the companions discover that they have in common some insight

each friend will the good of and for the other. Aristotle calls this willing of the good for another *goodwill*.

But even mutual goodwill is not enough to establish a friendship. Friendship also requires mutual recognition and reciprocity. If one person loves another, but the other does not know it, they will not be friends. Even if one person loves another, and the one loved does know about it, there will not be friendship unless the love is returned or reciprocated. Hence, friendship will be *an affective union of love between two persons that is mutually recognized and reciprocated.*

From this definition of friendship, it follows that friends must in some way be equal. For if two persons are so unequal that they cannot share a common good or make some kind of equal exchange, they will not fulfill the definition of friendship. There might be a semblance of friendship between parents and children, for example. But even in such cases, there is friendship to the degree that equality is found. Thus, the friendship between a parent and child is possible when the child approaches adulthood but not when the child is a tiny infant.

## The Kinds of Friendship

Since every friendship is based upon some common good, the kinds of friendships will be differentiated by the kinds of goods that are shared. A good can be a useful good, e.g., wealth and business partnerships are useful for providing the needs of life; a good can be a pleasant good, e.g., a funny conversation is a pleasant good; and a good can be good in itself, e.g., virtue and

---

or interest or even taste which the others do not share and which, till that moment, each believed to be his own unique treasure (or burden). The typical expression of opening Friendship would be something like, 'What? You too? I thought I was the only one'" (*The Four Loves* [San Diego, CA: Harcourt, Brace and Company, 1960], 96).

happiness are good in themselves. A good that is good in itself is often called the virtuous or noble good.

Corresponding to these three kinds of good are three kinds of friendship: the friendship of utility, the friendship of pleasure, and the friendship of virtue. Let us look at each one briefly.

A friendship of utility is a friendship in which each person finds the other useful for some other good. For example, two people might be friends because they are business partners and help one another gain wealth. Or one person might be good at academics, while the other is popular with the kids at school, so each gains something from the other by being friends: the one is helped to get better grades, while the other finds social acceptance. These friendships, while not necessarily bad, are very imperfect and really are founded upon love for oneself, not true love for the other. Once one of the friends ceases being useful, the friendship dissolves. So we can see that a friendship of utility falls short of the true notion of friendship: the useful friend is not really loved for his own sake.

A friendship of pleasure is a friendship in which each person finds the other pleasant to be around. For example, someone might enjoy their friend because he is funny and makes him laugh or because they enjoy playing sports together. Young men and women often form this kind of friendship because of the pleasures associated with romantic love. This kind of friendship is also imperfect since it does not involve loving the friend for his own sake but only for the sake of the pleasure he gives. Once one of them starts to be unpleasant to the other, the friendship dissolves. Even a young man and woman who think they truly love each other very quickly part ways when one becomes unpleasant and burdensome to the other.

A friendship of virtue is one in which each person desires that the other grow and remain in virtue. For example, two friends may help one another grow in wisdom or chastity or some such virtue. This kind of friendship is most truly called friendship since it involves loving the other person for his own sake. Virtue is the good of the other person, so by desiring virtue for him, someone loves his friend for his own good. Virtuous love is not self-directed. Such friendships are not dissolved easily since virtue is a stable habit. They are also long-lasting because even when one of the friends becomes no longer useful or turns unpleasant, the friendship remains intact since these things were not the reason for the friendship in the first place. A friendship of virtue is like a potential whole that includes both useful and pleasant friendships, for the friendship of virtue is also most useful for bringing about virtue and most pleasant since virtue is the most pleasing of goods. Thus, a friendship of virtue is the best form of friendship there is.

### Components of Friendship

Now that we understand it in general by the definition, we can see some of the parts that constitute what friendship truly is. Friendship begins with goodwill—it is the foundation of friendship. One can have goodwill toward another without being friends, but one cannot be friends with someone without extending to him goodwill. Following on this is concord, which is being in agreement or "of one mind" and having the same opinions on what is best, choosing the same actions, and resolving to do these things in common. Men who have concord enjoy working together, generally speaking, more than they do working apart; otherwise, it would be more useful than enjoyable. Finally, friendship is most excellently shown in beneficence, the giving of goods to others with no expectation or interest in making a return on the gift given. The beneficiary loves to give and to serve the beloved simply to give goodness to the other. In a friendship of virtue, the emphasis is placed on loving more than on being loved—clearly, love must be reciprocated by both parties, but it is the giving that shows the goodwill for no cause other than the person's goodness rather than being loved, which in itself is closer to being honored and is not something done for its own sake.

Two marks especially belong to friendship: friends must in some way be equal, and the act most proper to friendship is sharing a common life. Above all things, it is proper to friendship that friends desire to live together.

### Why Does Man Need Friendship to Be Happy?

If happiness is the perfect, self-sufficient good, it seems contradictory to say that the happy man needs anything. If someone has everything, he needs nothing. So it seems that the happy man does not need friends. But this argument misunderstands what is meant by self-sufficient when used to describe human happiness.

Aristotle often says that we are trying to understand human happiness, and therefore, we need to understand what is the greatest good for someone having a human nature. Human nature is not able to achieve happiness without help from other sources: the activity of contemplating God clearly depends upon God as an object of contemplation. But if a man suffers from poverty, illness, injury, or some other defect of bodily goods, this will also impede the activity of contemplation, as well as other virtuous activities. So while these external goods are not essentially part of happiness, they are instrumental in providing the conditions in which happiness can exist.

Friends are also important for the activities in which man experiences happiness. Some virtues can only be exercised together with friends. For example, social virtues pertaining to family life presuppose friendship between family members like husband and wife. Man is naturally a social animal, and so the ultimate perfection for a human being involves other human beings. But, in addition to this, Aristotle points out a striking fact of human life: we can observe the life and activities of others better than our own, and this increases the delight we experience when we see the virtuous life of a friend.

> Now we can study our neighbors better than ourselves, and their actions better than our own. Evidently then virtuous persons find pleasure in the actions of friends who are good men, since they have both qualities that are naturally pleasurable. The happy man, therefore, will need such friends inasmuch as he wants to study actions that are good and his own, and the actions of the virtuous man who is his friend are of this nature.[48]

Simple human experience verifies this observation of Aristotle. Consider the experience of going to the movies or to the zoo by yourself or with a good friend. Not only is the activity more enjoyable with a friend, but it is exceedingly more enjoyable. The virtuous friend gives us goodness to easily contemplate; both his person and his actions are worthy of thinking upon and what makes them lovable. It is far easier to contemplate external things than internal ones, and friends offer us the most joyful, proximate occasion for contemplating goodness, the ultimate end of man. Additionally, friends can serve as a mirror for ourselves.[49]

---

[48] *Nicomahean Ethics*, Bk. 9, lect. 10 (1170a1–4). *Commentary on Aristotle's Nicomachean Ethics*, 571. Tr. C.I. Litzinger, O.P., Dumb Ox Books, Notre Dame, Indiana, 1993.

[49] Christian revelation indicates that even God's happiness involves friendship among the three Persons of the Trinity. This harmonizes with our own

## Friendship with God?

This discussion of friendship leads to a question that is in part philosophical and in part theological. Can a man, or any creature for that matter, be friends with God? As we have already seen, friendship presupposes equality. Yet there seems to be little or no equality between man and God. In fact, God infinitely surpasses man in every good. Thus, it seems that there can be no truly common good between man and God and that there can be no true reciprocation between man and God, for what could a man offer to God in return for his entire being?

Considerations such as these lead Aristotle to conclude that friendship between man and God is impossible[50] (at least if friendship is understood in a strict sense). Yet, this seems to contradict Christian revelation, which asserts the possibility of friendship in a strict sense between man and God.[51]

This dichotomy is an example of a philosophical problem with a theological answer. Just as man has a natural desire to see the essence of God, but no active natural ability to do so, so too man has a natural desire for friendship with God but has no possibility of securing this good through his own abilities. Even Aristotle recognized the appropriateness of this seminal inclination in man:

> For if the gods have any care for human affairs, as it seems they do, it would be reasonable both that they should delight in that which was best and most akin to them (i.e., intellect) and that they should reward those

---

experience, which tells us that even if we had every good the way God does, we would still want friendship!

[50] See *Nicomachean Ethics*, Bk. 8, ch.7 (1159a6–7).

[51] See Jn 15:15.

> who love and honor this most, as caring for the things that are dear to them and acting both rightly and nobly.[52]

So philosophy has reached a kind of limit. There is in man a natural inclination to be friends with God, yet no power to be friends with God. Only divine revelation can answer this question. Yet that leads us from this text to another: the Christian New Testament. There it is asserted that God Himself confers upon man a share of His divine nature, making us in some way children and equals of God capable of sharing a common inheritance and good. We leave it to the reader to decide whether belief in such revelation satisfies the deepest longings of human reason. Philosophy must hold its peace.

**Summary**

- Friendship is an affective union of persons that is mutually recognized and reciprocated.
- The three kinds of friendship are friendships of utility, friendships of pleasure, and friendships of virtue.
- Of these, the friendship of virtue is most truly friendship.
- The act most proper to friendship is living together.
- A man cannot be fully happy without friends.
- If friendship between man and God is possible, it can only be so by God conferring upon man some kind of equality with Him.

52 *Nicomachean Ethics*, Bk. 10, ch. 8 (1179a24–9). Here Aristotle refers to immaterial substances as gods, so they include angels and God.

CHAPTER 9

# Education and Wisdom (the Return to Happiness)[53]

What does education have to do with happiness? Innumerable students from grade school to graduate school rejoice when they have a day off from school. Perhaps not all education is as it should be in the modern world, but even when education is defective, there are few who doubt the benefits of education. Before we examine the way in which education contributes to happiness, it is important to understand the true nature and purpose of education. The English word "education" is derived from the Latin expression *ex ducere* meaning "to lead out from." An education is supposed to lead someone out of a state of imperfection to a state of perfection.

Man is perfected by various virtues, and education is supposed to bring this perfection about by drawing these virtues forth from his soul. So education is not just academic in nature: it concerns both the intellectual and moral virtues. This naturally leads us to the question: What kind of education is best and most necessary?

[53] Supplementary texts: Peter Kreeft, *The Best Things in Life*, Chapter 2 "On Liberal Education and Careers" and Chapter 6 "On Success and the Greatest Good."

## The Definition of Education

To determine the best kind of education, it is first necessary to determine more distinctly what education is. As the origins of the word suggest, education is a kind of acting upon.[54] The educator acts upon the student to cause a change in the soul of the student. Since the change effected is in the soul, the student must freely cooperate with the educator. Ultimately, the student himself must bring this change about in his own soul. Since every agent acts for an end, it is also true that the educator will act for an end. This end is to perfect the soul of the student. And since the human soul is perfected by virtue, education can be defined as *acting upon a person in order to bring about the perfection of virtue in him.*

This "acting upon" is most effectively accomplished by way of good teaching (to bring about the intellectual virtues) and good example, together with discipline by means of fitting rewards and punishments (to bring about the moral virtues).

From this, it can be seen that the best education is the one that most effectively leads to the highest virtues. And since man's highest power is his reason, and since the greatest virtue of reason is wisdom, it follows that the best education is the one that leads toward wisdom.

## The Importance of Understanding Human Nature and Education Correctly

Notice how important it is to have a correct understanding of human nature in order to have a correct understanding of ethics in general and education in particular. As St. Thomas says in the introduction of his work *On Being and Essence*: "A small mistake in the beginning leads to a large mistake in the end." An error about

[54] In another sense, the motion itself in the soul of the one educated could also be called an education.

the nature of man will result in a mistake about what constitutes human perfection and about how men should act. For example, if one were to think falsely that man's highest perfection is found in making things (as Karl Marx thought), then an education in technology would be man's highest perfection. If one were to mistakenly think that man's highest perfection is found in the exercise of power (as Friedrich Nietzsche thought), then an education that teaches people how to gain power and influence (e.g., in politics) would be the best education. But as it is, none of these educations perfect man as man. It is one thing to be a good engineer or doctor and another thing to be a good man. It is one thing to be a good politician and another thing to be a good man. A good doctor or politician who is a bad man will end up doing much more harm than good to himself and to society and will ultimately be miserable, not happy, because he is not accomplishing the end of his nature as a human being. Therefore, it is essential that men pursue that education that perfects them first as men. Afterwards, they will be in a position to benefit themselves and society with training in some particular art or science.

The classical philosophical tradition that understood clearly that man is a rational animal perfected most of all by wisdom reflected upon the best education possible for man and concluded that an education in the traditional liberal arts,[55] completed by philosophy, is the best education for man. The liberal arts are those arts that free (from the Latin word *liber*) a man to come to know the highest truths.[56] Christian revelation has made it possible to seek

[55] Traditionally, there are seven liberal arts, divided into two parts. The trivium (grammar, logic, and rhetoric) is studied first, and then the quadriviium (geometry, arithmetic, astronomy, and music) follows after that.

[56] It is beyond the scope of this book to go into the liberal arts and explain how each contributes to human perfection; however, as a supplementary text the student may wish to read the founding document of Thomas Aquinas College in

more noble and perfecting education and an even higher wisdom through *sacred theology*. As a consequence, the absolutely best education for man is a Catholic education in the liberal arts that is ordered to the study of theology as its ultimate aim.

## Conclusion

Happiness is the goal of all our choices and actions. This happiness consists in the best reasonable activity. This best activity of reason involves knowing the best things in the best possible way so that we can understand happiness more distinctly as the activity of contemplating God by means of virtue, especially the best of the virtues. After an analysis of the various virtues and their relationship to one another, we concluded that the virtue of wisdom is the highest perfection of man's highest rational power. So in order to be happy, a man must successively acquire the virtues that ultimately lead to and make possible the virtue of wisdom.

This conclusion that wisdom is essentially connected with happiness manifests the importance of studying first philosophy (metaphysics), which comes at the end of philosophy. Moreover, education, in its best sense, is the road towards wisdom and hence, a privileged road towards happiness. Our study of ethics has returned to its beginning: What is the road we must follow to find happiness? Perhaps it is a road less traveled, ignored by most. But if it is the right road, following it will make all the difference.

## Summary

- An education is supposed to lead someone out of a state of imperfection to a state of perfection.
- For mankind, education's end is to perfect the soul of the student, both morally and intellectually.

---

California: *The Blue Book: A Proposal for the Fulfillment of Catholic Liberal Education.*

APPENDIX A

# Definitions for Ethics

*Ethics*: The art of acting in such a way as to best achieve the ultimate purpose of human life.

*Happiness* (*nominal*): The perfect (or ultimate) good of a rational being.

Or: That good for the sake of which everything is chosen and which is never chosen for the sake of anything else.

Or: That good that totally satisfies all desires.

*Happiness (essential)*: The activity of contemplating God by means of virtue.

*Moral Virtue*: A habit of choosing in the mean, according to reason and relative to us, as the prudent man would do.

*Choice*: A voluntary act as a result of deliberation, which determines the will to a single good means immediately within its power.

*Temperance*: The virtue of the concupiscible appetite that firmly inclines one to choose in the mean with regard to the pleasures of touch and taste so as to moderate the acts of nutrition and reproduction.

*Fortitude*: The virtue of the irascible appetite that firmly inclines one to choose in the mean with regard to fear and daring so as to strengthen one to persevere, especially in contests in which there is danger of death.

*Justice*: The virtue of the will that firmly inclines one to render to each person what is their due.

*Prudence*: Right reason about the things to be done (i.e., means to be chosen).

*Art*: Right reason about things to be made.

*Understanding*: The virtue of the mind by which the immediate and universal propositions are firmly grasped.

*Science*: The virtue of the mind by which the universal and necessary conclusions drawn from first, immediate propositions are firmly grasped.

*Wisdom*: The virtue of the mind by which one grasps the first and most universal causes of things and by which one judges all science and understanding.

*Friendship*: A mutual and affective love between two persons that is recognized by both and founded upon some shared good.

*Pleasure*: An act of an appetitive power that perfects the appetite as rest in a fitting good that is possessed.

APPENDIX B

# Civic and Family Life[57]

The "most complete" or "perfect" human community is that political community that has everything needed to actualize or fulfill man's highest natural abilities. If it did not possess these things, either there would be some other community that does possess them, and then this other community would be more perfect (and from this it would follow that there was something more perfect than the most perfect), or no community would possess the things necessary for actualizing man's highest natural abilities, and thus, nature would have endowed man with these abilities in vain. Since neither of these options is admissible, it follows that the most perfect human community is that political community that has everything needed to actualize or fulfill man's highest natural abilities.

Such a perfect community would not only provide the bare necessities needed for generation and survival but also those things necessary for man to live a perfect life according to reason and virtue. "The end of law and of a regime is not to dishearten [men], but to make men virtuous: and this is the end of politics."[58] This

[57] This appendix is an excerpt taken from a doctoral thesis by the author entitled: *The Primacy of the Common Good as the Root of Personal Dignity in the Doctrine of St. Thomas Aquinas*, Chapter 5.

[58] St. Thomas Aquinas, *Commentary on the Psalms*, 44, n. 5. See also his

is because that which is specific to and highest in human nature is reason. The perfection of man demands that the potencies of a rational nature be actualized to the highest possible degree, but for this to take place, it is necessary that all of those human faculties ordained to the perfect exercise of reason be actualized.

> To this, indeed, all other human activities seem to be ordained as to an end. Since, for the perfection of contemplation there is required soundness of body, to which are ordained all artificial things necessary for life. There is also required rest from the disturbances of the passions, to which one arrives through the moral virtues and prudence; and rest from external disturbances, to which is ordained the whole regimen of civil life. And so, if it be rightly considered, all human offices may be seen to serve the ones contemplating truth.[59]

When a political community is sufficiently large and well organized so as to provide the conditions and incentives necessary so that a life of reason and virtue can flourish among its citizens,

---

*Commentary on the Nicomachean Ethics.*, lect. 14: "The best of human goods, namely happiness, is the end of politics, whose end is manifestly operation according to virtue. For the political [art] strives for this principal endeavor by making laws and applying rewards and punishments, so that it might make good citizens and doers of good works. This is to act in accordance with virtue." Here it should be noted that St. Thomas is making reference to Aristotle's teaching. However, it is clear enough from other places in St. Thomas's writings that he is in fundamental agreement with Aristotle on this point. See, for example, *lectio* 19 of the same book.

[59] St. Thomas Aquinas, *Summa Contra Gentiles* (hereafter SCG), III. 37. Here again, contemplation should be taken in the sense of an act of the speculative intellect, motivated by love of the truth considered and accompanied by delight in that truth.

then such a community is a most perfect human community.[60] To the degree that a political community is deficient in these areas, it lacks the notion of a perfect community.[61]

Not every rational good is encompassed by the good common to the perfect political community.[62] This is so, first of all, because the political community is not something *per se* one. Its members have operations that do not pertain to the community as such. Secondly, the goods common among men must be communicated by way of external, sensible manifestations, for the internal thoughts and desires of a man's heart are not common or shared with other men unless they are expressed by some sensible manifestation.[63] Therefore, the political community is not directly concerned with the things held in secret in the human heart.[64] It

60 Among the organizations necessary for such a perfect community to exist would be, for example, educational institutions where human wisdom can be pursued in an orderly manner.

61 Of course, this is not to be understood as a kind of utopian civilization where, in fact, every person is provided with all the means necessary to achieve personal fulfillment. It suffices that a political community have all those civil organs that are indispensable for the acquisition of the moral and intellectual virtues, even if, for a given person or in a given case, the circumstances necessary for full human development are lacking. Needless to say, if a political community is to have the notion of a perfect community, it must be possible for at least some (and, ideally, as many as possible) of its citizens to arrive at the perfection of moral and intellectual virtue.

62 See STh., Ia–IIae, q. 21, a. 4, ad. 3: "Man is not ordained to the political community according to his whole self, and according to all that is his."

63 See STh., Ia–IIae, q. 91, a. 4, c: "The judgment of a man cannot be about interior motions which lie hidden, but only about exterior acts, which appear."

64 See St. Thomas Aquinas, *Commentary on Romans*, V, lect. 6: "The human law is referred to human judgment, which is about exterior acts. But the divine law is referred to the divine judgment, which is about the interior motions of the heart." See also STh., Ia–IIae, q. 98, a.1, c: "The end of human law is the temporal tranquility of the city, to which end the law arrives by restraining exterior acts with regard to those evils which can disturb the peaceful state of the city."

may be said that the dispositions and thoughts of the heart are the concern of the political community indirectly, but this is to the degree that such things are principles or effects of external actions or communications.[65] Thus, the legislator is interested in leading men to virtue principally because virtuous men tend to act and communicate with other men in such a way as to benefit the common good, while vicious men tend to do the opposite.[66] Therefore, when it is said that the aim of the political art is to make men virtuous, it should be understood that this is for the sake of a further end, namely the right order that virtuous men tend to establish in a community by their mutual interactions and communications. This right ordering of the community is nothing other than the concord of human society, which is the common good proper to the perfect political community.[67] This concord of human society is an order that removes the external impediments to the complete development and fulfillment of the human person.[68] More than this, it also provides needed incentives for the same. The reason for this is that since higher goods are less known to most men, it is natural for man to need certain enticements to pursue these higher goods. Such enticements are lower goods that are more proportioned and so more attractive to the one being enticed. In this way, the political art imitates

---

[65] See STh., Ia–IIae, q. 92, a. 1, ad. 1 and Ia–IIae, q. 99, a. 3, c.

[66] This is not to say that the legislator ought to be morally indifferent to whether men are actually virtuous. Even if, hypothetically, the identical external results could be obtained without making men virtuous, the legislator should choose that course that would produce real virtue since every man ought to be interested in the moral goodness of his fellow man.

[67] See SCG, III, 146.

[68] Such "external" impediments should not be understood to refer merely to impediments external to the community but rather external to the members of the community; besides invasion by foreign powers it would include, for example, internal civil strife or crime, extreme poverty, etc.

nature in which, for example, pleasure in eating is an enticement for achieving the greater good of nutrition, and sexual pleasure is used as an enticement to bring about the greater good of the propagation of the species.

Although the human person is not ordained to the good of the political community according to all that he is or has, nevertheless, this does not mean that the whole person is not ordained to the good of the political community. "The whole man is ordained, as to an end, to the whole community of which he is a part."[69] The reason for this is that the good of the political community is a good for the whole person and a good realized by the whole person,[70] even though it is not a good that completely exhausts (in the sense of fully actualizing) the natural potencies of the human person. Every part of a man, i.e., soul and body, and even the parts of the body, shares in the good of the political community, and every part of a man can be used for the building up of this common good. Thus, a man cannot dismember himself or take harmful drugs since he is not exclusively his own possession. When a man cuts off his hand, that hand can no longer be used to work for feeding and housing his family or combating foreign invaders in war. Because that part of him is no longer usable, others must suffer harm to their good since it is the common good that is compromised. That hand, and every part of a man, needs to be at the disposition of the political community of which a human person is a part.

Nevertheless, each part of a man need not be at the disposal of the political community at every time or in every respect. Sometimes, a man might use his hands simply to bring about a private good. Writing his diary, carving a piece of wood into

[69] STh., IIa–IIae, q. 65, a. 1.

[70] Indeed, this is true for every good that perfects human nature as such.

a pipe, and other such things are ordained for his private good. More importantly, a person need not direct all his thoughts or choices to the good of the political community. Indeed, if he were to do so, he would fail to actualize his highest natural abilities. His perfection would be compromised, for the good common to the perfect human community is not itself the realization of all the natural abilities of the human person, nor is it the object by which they might be realized. It is rather the foundation and condition for exercising the highest of these abilities. This good makes other, higher goods possible or even easier to attain,[71] but it does not, of itself, render them actual.[72]

Supreme among the activities to which man is ordained is the very act of contemplating truth. As we saw above, this is the actualization of man's highest natural ability. A person directs himself in this activity without being subject to the directives of the authority of the political community.[73] The simple reason

---

[71] In this respect we must disagree with certain positions proposed by M. Novak in which he seems to assert that political society has no positive role to play in the development of the human person in virtue as a preparation for the contemplation of truth and God; see *Free Persons and the Common Good* (New York: Madison Books, 1989), 4, 98. A view of political society that sees the role of the society as merely not obstructing the individual person's freedom for contemplation and for God is radically insufficient. The common good of political society is itself an end that falls within the order of ends natural to man, and therefore, it is not merely neutral, but it is positively ordained to the ultimate end.

[72] See J. Schall: "Political philosophy is in a sense necessary in order that we might have a polity that allows us to philosophize in the first place, a polity that recognizes its own incompleteness"; and a little later he states: "For St. Thomas, dealing with political things, with the law, with the regime, even with the best regime, is the first step to the freedom for confronting the divine things"; from "Political Philosophy: Remarks on its Relation to Metaphysics and Theology," *Angelicum*, 70 (1993), 504. For a more extended treatment of this relationship, see J. Pieper, *Leisure, the Basis of Culture*.

[73] See J. Maritain, *The Rights of Man and the Natural Law*, 17: "The community

for this is that the political authority does not have the capability to realize this kind of a good. "The highest good of man is not [achieved] in secular power."[74] The state is utterly powerless to bring about the good of the contemplation of truth in a human soul, and so it does not belong to its competency to give directives in such matters. Put another way, the causality of the common good of the political community (as a final cause) is not capable of drawing forth or actualizing the activity of the contemplation of truth. For this, a common good of a higher order is necessary. The end of the speculative intellect is a good higher than the good that can be achieved in the political or any practical order.

> Someone, from the fact that he is speculating, is himself directed singularly unto the end of speculation. However, the end itself of the speculative intellect exceeds the good of the practical intellect as much as its singular attainment exceeds the common attainment of the good of the practical intellect. And therefore, the most perfect beatitude consists in [the act of] the speculative intellect.[75]

This is nothing other than to say that the political community is ordained to an end beyond itself. This end beyond the good of the political community is not the singular activity of contemplation of the individual persons but rather the common object of

---

is entitled to expect the mathematician to serve the social group by *teaching* mathematics. . . . But the community will never have the right to require the mathematician *to hold as true* some one mathematical system rather than any other, or to teach such mathematics as is deemed to be more in conformity with the law of the social group."

[74] *SCG*, III. 31.

[75] St. Thomas Aquinas, *Commentary on the Sentences*, Bk. IV, d. 49, q. 1, a. 1c, ad. 1.

contemplation shared by the members of the community.[76] This common object is the natural order (or some part of it) and the cause of this order, namely God.[77]

From the foregoing, therefore, it can be readily seen that the good of the perfect political community is a good that brings the members of that community into a state of proximate potency to the contemplation of truth. "The active life is a disposition for the contemplative life."[78] That is, full participation in the common good of the perfect human community prepares the human person to enter more fully into the common good of the whole universe. Joseph Pieper sums this up well.

> All practical activity, from the practice of the ethical virtues to gaining a means of livelihood, serves something other than itself. And this other thing is not practical activity. It is having what is sought after, while we rest content in the results of our active efforts. Precisely that is the meaning of the old adage that the *vita activa* is fulfilled in the *vita contemplativa*. To be sure, the active life contains a felicity of its own; it lies, says Thomas, in the practice of prudence, in the perfect art of the conduct of life. But the ultimate repose cannot be found in this kind of felicity. *Vita*

76 See De Koninck, *De la Primauté du Bien Commun,* 61: "The practical happiness of the community is not, through itself, ordained to the speculative happiness of the singular person, but to the speculative happiness of the person insofar as he is a member of the community."

77 If the term "contemplation" is used in the strictest sense, it applies to the consideration of God in Himself, while the inspection of divine things in and by created things is called speculation (see St. Thomas Aquinas, *Commentary on the Sentences*, Bk. III, d. 35, q. 1, a. 2c, c).

78 St. Thomas Aquinas, *Commentary on the Sentences*, Bk. III, d. 35, q. 1, a. 3c, c. See S.T., IIa–IIae; q. 181, a.1, ad. 3.

> *activa est dispositio ad vita contemplativa*; the ultimate meaning of the active life is to make possible the happiness of contemplation.[79]

The political community that we have outlined above is itself composed of smaller communities of persons, of which the most fundamental and important is the natural family. Like the other integral wholes that we have already considered, the family has a unity of order only. Therefore, its intrinsic good will likewise be the order and peace of the family.

Peace and order are established in a family when justice is observed among its members. Justice, however, concerns what is due to each. Since the members of a family are unequal (as, for example, parent and child), it follows that the just for each is not the same. It is not our intention here to provide a detailed explanation of the various communications and actions that establish right order in a family. Indeed, this would merit a thesis of its own.[80] Here, we simply intend to identify the principal good common to the family as such and the chief acts and means by which it is promoted and preserved.

A first observation is that the common goods upon which a family is based pertain to the necessities of life, such as generation and nutrition.[81] It is a fact of human experience that families come together most often for these reasons. For example, meals are nearly always at the center of family gatherings, and parents frequently come to visit their children, even those who are far away, to help

---

[79] "The Purpose of Politics," in *Joseph Pieper: An Anthology* (San Francisco: Ignatius Press, 1989), 121.

[80] For a survey of the principal kinds of relationships and common goods involved in the family unit see *Nicomachean Ethics*, VIII, 12.

[81] See St. Thomas Aquinas, *Commentary on the Nicomachean Ethics*, Bk. VIII, lect. 12: "Domestic society is ordered to the acts necessary for life, namely generation and nutrition."

care for a newborn child. Such goods are not among the most noble goods, but they are the most fundamental, and a large part, if not the greater part, of human life is often spent attending to these necessities. For example, a husband may work through the day to provide food, shelter, and clothing for the family, and a wife may attend to the maintenance of the house, the preparation of meals, and the care of the children. Moreover, since the most immediate needs of life are acquired through external possessions, it happens that one of the principal proximate aims of family life is the acquisition and maintenance of goods,[82] which are used as instruments to achieving peace and a well-ordered life in the family.[83]

Since the human child needs more than nutrition to come to full maturity, it is also necessary that the basic elements of a moral and intellectual formation be communicated to the children by the parents. "Nature does not intend only the generation [of the child], but the support and upbringing to the perfect state of a man, as man, which is the state of virtue. Hence, according to the Philosopher, we have three things from parents: namely being, nutrition, and education."[84] Children learn to speak and recognize the first elements of rational discourse in the family. Through the discipline, instruction, and example of their parents and older siblings, they receive their first formation in moral character. So foundational is this first moral formation that it caused Aristotle to remark that "it makes a very great difference, or rather all the difference."[85]

---

82 See St. Thomas Aquinas, *On Kingship*, I. 15.

83 See St. Thomas Aquinas, *Commentary on the First Epistle to Timothy,* III, lect. 2: "The good administration [of a family] is not only the acquisition of riches, since these are not the end of household administration, but the instruments. Yet its end is a rectified life: Sir. 44:6, 'making peace within his family.'" As an old adage says: "When there's no hay, the donkeys fight."

84 St. Thomas Aquinas, *Commentary on the Sentences*, Bk. IV, d. 26, q. 1, a. 1, c.

85 *Nicomachean Ethics*, II. 1, 1103b25.

Children, on their part, chiefly owe honor, obedience, and gratitude to their parents: honor since the parents are a principle of their coming to be and of their sustenance, especially in the first years of life, and honor is nothing other than a recognition of superiority and excellence in another;[86] obedience since the parents have care of the common good of the family, in which the children cannot share without being subject to the will of those who have care of this good;[87] and gratitude since it is clearly contrary to reason to be ungrateful for having received such great goods.[88]

Briefly, these are the kinds of acts and communications by which order is established, fostered, and preserved within family society. When family members, to the degree that they are able, render to one another what is due in these areas, the family remains at peace. When any of these is lacking to a large degree, the family order is disrupted, especially when the disorder pertains to the most fundamental of these acts, the act of generation, which is at the center of the relation between husband and wife as well as parents and children.

The communication of the kinds of goods we have outlined above depends heavily upon the bonds of natural love that are established by the act of generation that is so central to family life.[89] Indeed, in virtue of this act, the persons themselves become

---

[86] See St. Thomas Aquinas, *Commentary on the Nicomachean Ethics,* Bk. VIII, lect. 11: "For since the father is superior, it follows that parents are honored by their children. For honor is due to a superior."

[87] See St. Thomas Aquinas, *Commentary on the Epistle to the Ephesians*, VI, lect. 1: "Fathers are naturally obliged to instruct their children in morality, but children, when they are instructed by their parents, are naturally obliged to obey them, just as the sick ought to obey a doctor. Hence, obedience is proper to children."

[88] See STh., IIa–IIae, q. 106, a. 1.

[89] See St. Thomas Aquinas, *De Virtutibus*, q. 2, a. 7, c.

the common good of the other members of the family. The children are the common good of both parents;[90] each parent is a good common to all of their children.[91] This natural love is not merely based upon choice (even though it may be perfected by choice) but is founded in the natural relation established between parents and offspring.[92] There is a certain sense in which parents cannot do otherwise than love their children, and children cannot do otherwise than love their parents. Experience shows that the need to love and be loved by family members goes far beyond the need to love and be loved by those who are our friends by choice. Without this foundation of natural love, the unity and order of the family life is compromised.

In relation to the common good of political society as a whole, it is obvious that the goods provided by the family society are necessary foundations of and stepping stones to the good that the political community intends to realize. The first formation in moral and intellectual virtue provided by the family is presupposed to the integration of persons into the larger civic community. Precisely because of its natural bonds and limited size, the family unit is

---

[90] See St. Thomas Aquinas, *Commentary on the Nichomachean Ethics*, Bk. VIII, lect. 12: "Children are the common good of both, namely of the husband and the wife, whose conjunction is for the sake of offspring."

[91] See St. Thomas Aquinas, *Commentary on the Nichomachean Ethics*, Bk. VIII, lect. 12: "Children have friendship for parents as for a kind of superexcellent good."

[92] See St. Thomas Aquinas, *Commentary on the Nichomachean Ethics*, Bk. VIII, lect. 12: "Parents love their children for the reason that they are something of them. For children are procreated from the seed of their parents. Hence, a son is in a certain way a part of the father separated from him. Thus, this friendship is closest to that love by which someone loves himself, from which all friendship is derived, as is said in the ninth book [of the *Nicomachean Ethics*]. Reasonably, therefore, is paternal friendship put down as the principle. But children love their parents insofar as they have being from them, just as a separated part would love the whole from which it is separated."

better able to inculcate moral virtue and establish the foundations of intellectual virtue.[93] One need only imagine a scenario where the state was responsible for the care of all persons immediately from birth to see clearly how necessary the family unit is as the foundation of political society. Even when such institutions as orphanages become necessary due to circumstances in some cases, the aim of such institutions is to provide transitional care for children until they can be adopted by families. The family is simply a better instrument that is more proportioned to the individual person for realizing, in all their concrete detail, these more foundational goods.[94] Thus, for example, in accordance with the principle of subsidiarity, according to which that which can be done well or better through a lesser authority should be left to that lesser authority, parents have the obligation and right to be the first educators of their children.

It is only when parents fail gravely in this obligation that the state has the right and duty to intervene. An insightful passage from Aristotle's *Nicomachean Ethics* reveals the importance of the natural bonds of familial love to the well-being of the political community. "For as in cities, laws and prevailing types of character have force, so in households do the injunctions and the habits of the father; and these have even more, because of the tie of blood

[93] Pontifical Council for the Family, *The Charter of Rights of the Family*, preamble (Vatican City: *Liberia Editrice Vaticana*, 1983): "The family constitutes, much more than a mere juridical, social or economic unit, a community of love and solidarity, which is uniquely suited to teach and transmit cultural, ethical, social, spiritual, and religious values."

[94] V. Bachelet, "L'educazione al Bene Commune," in *Atti della XXXVI Settimana Sociale dei Cattolici d'Italia* (Rome: *Scuola Typografica Don Orione*, 1965), 223: "The first instrument for the education in the meaning of the common good in all its dimensions is certainly always the family."

and the benefits he confers: for the children start with a natural affection and disposition to obey."[95] St. Thomas comments:

> A paternal precept does not have the full coercive force of the precept of a king, as was said above. But, consequently, he shows that, in some respect, this [supervision] befits a private person more than a public one, due to kinship and benefits, on account of which children love their parents, and obey from a natural facility of friendship, which exists between children and their father. Therefore, although the precept of the king may be more powerful by way of fear, nevertheless, the paternal precept is more powerful through the way of love, which way is more efficacious in those who are not completely ill disposed.[96]

At the same time, it must be recognized that the larger political society is necessary for the well-being[97] of the family. "The proper good of any single person cannot exist without *economia*, that is, the right disposition of the family, nor without civic prudence, that is, the right disposition of the city, just as the good of the part is not able to exist without the good of the whole."[98] Thus,

[95] *Nicomachean Ethics*, X. 9, 1180b5. The entire ninth chapter of book ten includes a number of insightful observations on the principle of subsidiarity. Consider, for example, the following passage taken from the same chapter: "A boxer presumably does not prescribe the same style of fighting for all his pupils. It would seem then that the detail is worked out with more precision if the control is private; for each person is more likely to get what suits his case."

[96] St. Thomas Aquinas, *Commentary on the Nicomachean Ethics*, Bk. X, lect. 15.

[97] Here we make reference to the classic distinction between *necessitas ad esse* and *necessitas ad bene esse* found in *Metaphysics*, V.5. See St. Thomas Aquinas, *Commentary on the Sentences*, Bk. IV, d. 7, q. 1, a. 1b, c.

[98] St. Thomas Aquinas, *Commentary on the Nicomachean Ethics*, Bk. VI, lect. 7. See STh., IIa–IIae, q. 47, a. 10, ad. 2.

for example, the family needs assistance in the correction of the criminally malicious through the coercive power of the state. Or again, there is need for defense from outside aggressors by means of national defense. Not only this, but the perfections of higher education and the acquisition of all of the things necessary for living well would be impossible for a solitary family or even for a small group of families. As a result of this, even the limited education and provisions made for children according to the proper scope of the family would be significantly compromised if the family itself did not live within a larger, self-sufficient political community. The family and civil society have a complementary role in realizing the common good of the human person.[99]

In relation to the larger whole of the entire universe, the family also provides remote preparation for sharing in the good common to the whole universe, for that soundness of body which is necessary to engage in the contemplative life depends largely upon the proper nutrition obtained in the family environment. Moreover, it is principally in the family that the moral virtues that free a person from excessive internal disturbances of the passions are planted and developed. These virtues, in turn, together with the elementary intellectual virtues that have their origin in the family, make a person better disposed for the contemplation of that universal order, according to which created persons most fully partake of the good common to the whole universe.

Because of its foundation in nature and its natural ordination to a good beyond even the good of the perfect human community,

[99] "The family and society, which are mutually linked by vital and organic bonds, have a complementary function in the defense and advancement of the good of every person and of humanity." From the preamble to *The Charter of Rights of the Family*.

namely the good of the entire human race,[100] it follows that a number of significant aspects of the family society are not wholly subject to the positive laws of the political community.[101] This is simply to recognize that the family, as a kind of work of nature, has a fundamental structure and essential properties determined by the order that reason discovers in nature, an order we have briefly sketched above. Laws that, though they seem to be expedient for a given state at a given time, do not respect this natural order of the family society are, in fact, not laws at all[102] since they do not accord with right reason, nor can they genuinely contribute, *per se*, to the welfare of the state. It must be stressed that if there is anything in the family that escapes the competence of the larger whole that is the perfect human community, it is only because it pertains immediately to a higher order of goods, either the intrinsic common good or separated common good of the universe. The primacy of the common good has universal validity.

It is clear from the foregoing that the common good of the family provides a disposition for and is ordered to the common good of the whole political community, for the benefits that accrue from a well-ordered family life place a person in proximate potency to enter into political society by preparing the person to receive more fully its benefits and to contribute more effectively to realizing its good.

---

[100] See STh., IIa–IIae, q. 154, a. 2, c: "Sexual union is ordained to the good of the whole human race."

[101] From the preamble to *The Charter of Rights of the Family:* "The family, a natural society, exists prior to the state or to any other community, and possesses inherent rights which are inalienable."

[102] STh., Ia–IIae, q. 92, a. 1, ad. 4: "A tyrannical law, since it is not according to reason, is not simply speaking a law, but is rather a certain perversion of law."